BILLINGHAM

PAUL MENZIES

The History Press

I would like to dedicate this book to: my wife Jackie Menzies, who is always there for me; Keith Kirtley, a 'Billingham friend' for over half a century; my father, Bob Menzies, one of the newcomers who arrived in Billingham in 1929, and to Dr Lara Menzies, Dr James Pickett, Steve and Matthew Robinson, who are part of our future.

First published 2008

The History Press
The Mill, Brimscombe Port
Stroud, Gloucestershire, GL5 2QG
www.thehistorypress.co.uk

Reprinted 2009, 2011, 2012, 2013

British Library Cataloguing in Publication Data.
A catalogue record for this book is available from the British Library.

ISBN 978 0 7524 4838 1

Typesetting and origination by The History Press
Printed and bound in Great Britain by
Marston Book Services Limited, Didcot

CONTENTS

Acknowledgements   4

Introduction   5

Bibliography   8

1   Billingham in 1900   9

2   Farms and other places   23

3   Life at Billingham Hall   37

4   Green fields no more   53

5   Growing up   69

6   On the map   89

7   Life on the farm   103

8   Expanding again   115

ACKNOWLEDGEMENTS

I give grateful thanks to all those individuals and organisations that have allowed me to copy and use their material, given of their time and generally helped in my research. I have taken a great deal of time in tracing and establishing ownership of all material and ensuring that permission for reproduction in this work has been given, whether in copyright or not.

Permission to include material including images, map extracts and written material has been given by the late Alan Bell, the late Freda Bell-Moulang, the late Leslie Dixon, Bob Edwards, Peter Fletcher, Ivan Harrington, Helen Hay, the family of the late Eddie Hutton, R.C. Menzies, the late Bill Skeldon, the late Elizabeth Smith, Dr Kenneth Cecil Warne, Julian Harrop at the ICI Collection at Beamish Museum, Jo Faulkner at Stockton on Tees Borough Council Museums Service, Steve Wild at Stockton Reference Library, Middlesbrough Reference Library, David Tyrell and Janet Baker at Teesside Archives, Alan Sims at the *Evening Gazette*, Teesside, Joy Yates at the *Hartlepool Mail*, Steve Hearn at the Ordnance Survey and Jonathan Pepler at the Cheshire and Chester Archives and Local Studies, Chester. The original images of the building of the Synthetic Ammonia & Nitrates Limited factory are deposited with Cheshire and Chester Archives and Local Studies and are reproduced with the permission of Cheshire County Council and Chester City Council and that of the owner with whom copyright is reserved. Other material is from the author's own collection.

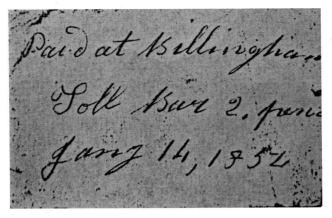

This is an example of a toll ticket costing two pence; it was issued on 14 January 1854 at Billingham Toll Bar and allowed the purchaser to use the Turnpike between Billingham and Norton. It is said that a couple of horses were always kept at Toll Bar Cottage in case anyone required assistance getting up Billingham Bank.

INTRODUCTION

It is with some astonishment that I find it is nearly thirty years since I began researching my first book about Billingham. Many of the people whom I interviewed then have since passed away. The memories they left behind were always of importance, but now they are priceless. As I sit listening to those people talking in the interviews taped all those years ago, it is a remarkable experience to be taken back to a time when Billingham was a village green surrounded by houses and a few isolated outlying farms. The voices of the interviewees even sound different from those voices of people in Billingham today. I am referring to their more rural accents as well as what they talked about. Their vocabulary is different, featuring words like 'forty acre', 'smithy', 'hoss n' cart', or 'hay-mekin', words that the residents from modern housing estates in Billingham would normally associate with rural communities.

But of course, that was what Billingham was in 1900 – a rural community with a history going back over 1,000 years. Many people worked within the village as farmers or agricultural workers, or in a service occupation. Some never ventured outside the village and, even if they did, it was only as far as Stockton to the annual Hiring Fair in order to hire farm servants or to secure employment for themselves for the next few months. Few people alive today will remember those days, a time before the First World War. The First World War certainly changed history, but for the people of Billingham it wasn't the war that changed their lives forever – it was the arrival of industry on a scale previously unknown to them.

Although this work is specifically neither a social nor an economic history, it touches on aspects of both genres. Any assessment of Billingham and its development during the last 100 years will show that the two are very much intertwined and impossible to separate. This was a time when those who lived in Billingham had very different priorities to those who live there today – or did they? One thing that I have discovered in researching history is that people are essentially the same whatever the era in which they are living. Humour, tragedy, hope and despair can always be found in the events which create the history of our society.

In researching this book, I have listened to and read about the lives of many people. Through all of their stories there runs a series of core values which form a part of the history of Billingham. Only a few snippets from their lives can be included here. In any case, this work is not a history of Billingham; it is a collection of images drawn from a variety of sources which, supported by oral and written evidence, can begin to give an insight into the origins of the town that we know today. Whatever else is true, Billingham as we know it is not the Billingham that its inhabitants in 1900 would recognise.

In particular the images look at the developments and changes that have occurred in Billingham since it began its inexorable transition from rural village, unknown outside its own local region, to a town known throughout the country and indeed the world through its association with ICI. It is hoped that this work may assist in the preservation of some aspects of the life of that former village community and, in doing so, ensure that some evidence will always be available for perusal by those who are curious about it in the future.

One of the more pleasing aspects of my return to researching the history of Billingham has been the discovery of new evidence about the development of the town. A greater awareness now exists of the importance of the past – personal history as well as the history of organisations and the communities in which they operate. Thirty years ago my interest in the history of Billingham would often provoke a surprise reaction; usually along the lines of 'What do you want to know that for?' Images, in particular, were few and far between and hard to find. Even large companies like ICI had only a very basic archive, much of it not catalogued nor centrally based but spread far and wide. This seemingly rather uncaring attitude was not a deliberate policy of neglect; rather it was just that neither people nor organisations considered it very important to preserve ephemera from the past. Thankfully, this attitude has now totally changed and people are more likely to preserve such material, even if only because it has become valuable in its own right (topographical postcards, for example). Where once there was just a biscuit tin full of random, unlabelled old negatives, now there are thriving internet sites which allow for the inspection of primary and secondary sources from anywhere in the world.

Writing this book has been an experience rich in the joys of discovery. The research, which, as ever, has consumed a great deal of time, has been a tale not only of instant access to material on the internet, but also the more traditional task of spending whole days, or even weeks, going through boxes of dusty artefacts from the past. In particular, my discoveries of new material concerning Billingham Hall and the early days of Synthetic a & Nitrates Ltd has been very exciting, especially as I was of the belief that most of this sort of evidence had long been destroyed.

As ever, I must pay tribute to those who facilitated this process, all of whom gave unstintingly of their time. Helen Hay, whose mother lived at Billingham Hall, deserves my sincere thanks for allowing me to peruse her family archives once again – just as she did twenty-five years ago. She has been a model of patience and kindness in giving me the information for the chapter in this book which explores her family life in the early 1900s.

Ivan Harrington, 'photographer extraordinaire', deserves a huge thank you. He very kindly shared some of his photographic archive with me and allowed me to use his material for this work. In addition, he very patiently gave me invaluable information about his family and their lives at Pond House.

Dr Kenneth C. Warne, now aged 102, is a remarkable man with an incredibly detailed memory of the days in 1922 when he first began work at Synthetic Ammonia & Nitrates Ltd. I found it truly fascinating to talk to someone who was a part of those far-off, pioneering days, a time when walking from one office to another often meant tramping across muddy farm fields. To think that he was personally associated with the men who created that industrial miracle is quite awesome. Dr Warne's association with Synthetic Ammonia & Nitrates Ltd and ICI encompassed his years at the University of Frankfurt in the early 1930s. To listen to him sharing his memories of those days when he was such a close observer of events which changed the world, would, in itself, have made my time spent on this project worthwhile. To Dr Warne I owe a huge debt of gratitude.

Other individuals whom I need to mention include several from organisations that made information and evidence available for me to use. These include Julian Harrop at Beamish Museum, Jonathan Pepler at Cheshire Archives, Jo Faulkner at Stockton Museum Service,

Alan Sims at the *Evening Gazette*, Joy Yates at the *Hartlepool Mail*, the staff at Middlesbrough Reference Library, David Tyrell and Janet Baker, stalwarts of Teesside Archives, Steve Wild at Stockton Library, Bob Edwards, R.C. Menzies, the Ordnance Survey organisation, British Rail (as it then was), York, and, of course, Cate Ludlow at The History Press, who was the instigator of this work.

There are a number of individuals who assisted me or provided evidence thirty years ago, material that I am able to use again in this work. They include Peter Fletcher – whose book, *Billingham in Bygone Village Days*, gives an excellent account of life in Billingham in the early 1900s – Ronnie Fletcher, Mike Hoare, the Moon family, the Addison family, J.W. Chesney and Donald Blakely. I would also like to thank Julian Philips for his help and the many stimulating conversations we have had about the history of ICI.

Last, but certainly not least, I would like to mention those people with whom I spent time collecting evidence from thirty years ago and who have since passed away. By sharing their life stories, they and their memories are not forgotten. My debt to all those mentioned below is immense. They include Leslie Dixon, with whom I shared many moments of laughter, Bill Skeldon, who shared so much material with me, Harry Briggs, who gave me an perceptive insight into Edwardian Billingham, Freda Bell-Moulang, who gave me an insight into her idyllic childhood spent on High Grange Farm, Alan Bell, her brother, for his memories and for allowing me to use so much of his photographic collection, Charles Wreford Hay, Grace Beatrice Menzies, and Elizabeth 'Betty' Smith, all of whom provided memories for me to use. I have attempted to contact surviving relatives of those mentioned. Where I have been unable to do so, I hope that word of mouth will bring this work to their attention.

Similarly, whilst I have attempted to ensure that there are no obvious mistakes in this work, I would like to apologise in advance for any errors that have been made, factual or otherwise. Please let me know of any errors and I will update my records. In the same vein, if anyone has any more information or evidence about the history of Billingham that they would like to share with me please get in touch, especially if you have any images that you will allow me to copy. With computer technology they can be copied in minutes and, in the case of damaged material, they can even be restored to a state which may even be an improvement on the original print! I have been pleased to provide digitally-restored images for a number of people. Also, in digitally preserving these images they are being saved in a form where they will not deteriorate.

Writing of any nature always impacts on those people closest to you and this is the case here. I would like to offer an enormous thank you to my dear wife Jackie, who has had to put up with many months of my rising at 5 a.m. to write before going off to work, as well as many rainy afternoons spent at the Reference Library in Middlesbrough. To her I owe a debt which I can never repay.

Finally, many of these images have been digitally restored using Photoshop Elements. In doing so, the sole aim has been to restore each image as closely as possible to its original state when first printed. Occasionally, in performing digital restoration, decisions have to be taken to include something which does not exist – for example, a missing part of an image. It is hoped that where this is the case you will agree the image has been sensitively restored – indeed, I hope you will not even be able to tell!

Paul Menzies
m.menzies1@ntlworld.com

BIBLIOGRAPHY

Books

Bamforth, H., et al, *Billingham Port Clarence and Haverton Hill in 1851* (Durham University: Durham, 1975)
Betteney, A., *The Brickworks of the Stockton-on-Tees Area* (Tees Valley Heritage Group: Teesside, 2007)
Chapman, V., *Around Billingham* (Chalford: Stroud, 1996)
Fletcher, P., *Billingham in Bygone Village Days* (Peter Fletcher: Billingham, 1987)
Fordyce, W., *A History of Coal, Coalfields and Iron Manufacture in Northern England* (Sampson Low and Co., London, 1860)
Harrison, J.W.H., *A Survey of the Lower Tees Marshes* (publisher unknown: 1916)
Hatton, C.H., *Haverton Hill, Port Clarence to Billingham* (Tempus: Stroud, 2005)
Marchant, A., Marchant, J., *Tithe Maps of Hartness* (Christian Inheritance Trust: Yarm, 1995)
Marchant, A., Marchant, J., *Billingham St Cuthbert, Clergymen of Cleveland* (Christian Inheritance Trust: Yarm, 1993)
Marchant, A., Marchant, J., *Billingham Church History* (Christian Inheritance Trust: Yarm, 1993)
Mathews, E., *Cassel Works* (ICI: Billingham, 1980)
Menzies, P., *Billingham in Times Past* (Countryside: Chorley, 1985)
Menzies, P., *Billingham in Times Past Vol. 2* (Countryside: Chorley, 1986)
Parkes, V.E., *Billingham – the first Ten Years* (ICI: Billingham, 1957)
Philips, J., *A Brief History of the Chemical Industry on Teesside* (TCI: Middlesbrough, 1999)
Philips, J., *A Short History of ICI at Billingham* (ICI: Billingham, 1986)
Still, L., Southern, J., *The Medieval Origins of Billingham* (Billingham Urban District Council: Billingham, 1968)
University of London, *The Victoria History of the Counties of England* (Dawsons: London, 1968)

Articles in Periodicals

Blench, E.A., 'The Billingham Enterprise', in *Chemistry and Industry*, July and August 1958
Howes, P., 'The Inter-War Development of Billingham', in *Cleveland and Teesside Local History Society Bulletin 53*, Autumn 1987

Other Sources

Ancestry website, ancestry.co.uk, Births, Marriages and Deaths Index, Military Records 1914-1918, Census Records 1841-1901
Billingham Express, various editions from 1952 to 1966, available on microfiche at Middlesbrough Reference Library
Billingham Press, various editions from 1946 to 1952, available on microfiche at Middlesbrough Reference Library
Billingham South School, *Log Book 1931-1984*, Durham County Council (1984)
Billingham Urban District Council, *Programme for opening of Council Offices* (1930)
Billingham Urban District Council, *Council Handbook* (1968)
Evening Gazette, Teesside, editions from 1899 to 1968, available at Middlesbrough Reference Library
Hartlepool Mail, photographic material held at Teesside Archives
Interview notes for 'Sixty-Five Years of ICI', an exhibition held by Stockton Museum Service (1991)
Norton Heritage Group, *The Old Billingham Walk* (Norton: 2004)
Norton Heritage Group, *Billingham c. 790-1948* (Norton: 1983)
Ordnance Survey, 6 inch series, Sheets 44, 45, 50, 51 (1857, 1897, 1916)
Ordnance Survey, 25 inch series, Sheets 44, 45, 50, 51 (1857, 1897, 1916)
Stockton and Teesside Herald, various editions from 1919 to 1940, available on microfiche at Middlesbrough Reference Library
Stockton Local History Journal, *Notes on Teesside Rail Stations* (April 2006)
Stockton Museums Service, *Discover Cowpen Bewley* (Stockton Borough Council, 2007)
Stockton Museums Service, various ephemera from the opening of Billingham Council Offices (1930)
The Times, online archive 1785-1985 (Times Newspapers, 2008)
Various oral interviews conducted between 1978 and 2008, typed up as statements of individual memories
In addition a large number of Trade Directories for County Durham and North Yorkshire, covering the period 1828 to 1939, have been consulted and used to provide and verify information.

1

BILLINGHAM IN 1900

This image encapsulates the two worlds, the old and the new, that made up Billingham in the early twentieth century. The top part of the image is a view of the village across Billingham Green looking towards the open fields of Billingham Grange and Tibbersley Farms. It was on this land that most of the initial industrial development would occur, changing its physical appearance forever. In 1918 the Ministry of Munitions began the construction of their proposed nitrates factory which would eventually become the huge industrial complex of ICI. In the lower part of the image the nightwatchman, Robert Marlow, is shown at the site in its early days.

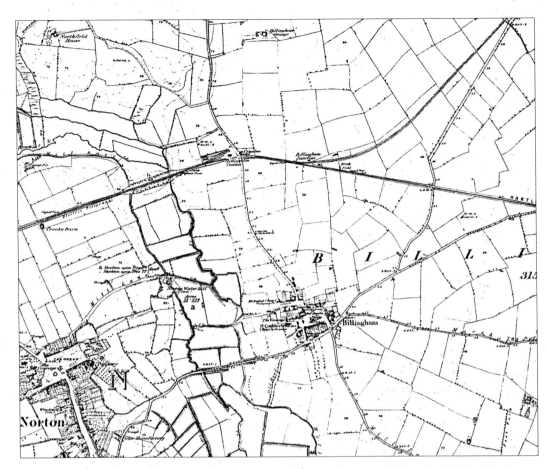

Billingham in 1900 was a self-contained community with a growing sense of identity. This is evident from the minutes of the parish council, created in 1894. Billingham Green, the village centre, was surrounded by labourers' cottages and some larger residences for the more wealthy. Most land was still used for mixed farming; the only industries of any note were the salt and iron works at Haverton Hill and Port Clarence. The community was completed by a number of outlying farms, an ancient watermill and some large new 'country dwellings' – close to Billingham railway station but distant from the village. One main road passed through Billingham linking Stockton, the nearest town, with Sunderland. An Act of Parliament in 1789 created a Turnpike Trust charged with 'altering, raising, widening, repairing and preserving... the road'. This involved redirecting the road across Billingham Bottoms, an important advance, and Old Road, the previous route, now became disused by all but a few villagers anxious to avoid paying the toll. In the early nineteenth century the *Mail*, the *Pilot* and the *Expedition* stagecoaches still passed daily through the village. Other less important roads from the village included Marsh Lane, leading to Billingham Grange and Tibbersley Farm, and Mill Lane, which went to Brook House Farm and Billingham Mill. Neither lane went any further – only marshland and the river lay beyond. Another lane forked soon after leaving the village. One fork, a road to Middle Belasis Farm and the ancient Belasis Hall, then became a footpath to Haverton Hill. The other, a lonely track to Cowpen Bewley, crossed the Clarence Railway at Cowpen Lane Gate. The opening of this railway in 1833 had little local impact initially, probably because it was located some distance to the north of the village. It was also for freight, rather than passenger traffic. (Reproduced from 1857 Ordnance Survey map, 6 inch series, with the kind permission of the Ordnance Survey)

Most people lived around Billingham Green. This view from around 1901 shows, on the left, labourers' cottages on North Row built in the 1870s. East Row, with its mainly eighteenth-century buildings, is dominated by Brewery House with its tall chimney. Between North Row and Brewery House lies School House, built in 1898, and a 'Thompson'-style farmhouse. Beyond Brewery House are Village and Town End Farms. The green is divided by the road with Parish Green to the left whilst to the right is Common Green which was used by villagers for grazing their animals.

This exceptionally clear image was obtained from a series of glass negatives from around 1894. The poor state of the road, often a subject for debate at parish council meetings, is very apparent. Henry Eldon Fletcher's Billingham Cash Trading Stores and the National School dominate the scene. The village cross and one of the village water pumps are also visible. Brewery House and Village Farm are in the distance. The lack of lighting, another much debated point at meetings of the parish council, can be seen here.

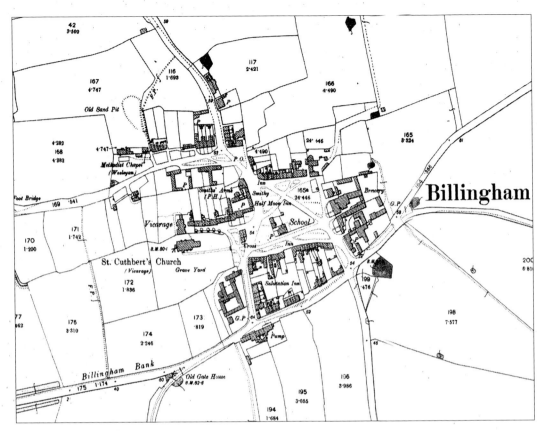

The images in this chapter can be located on this 1897 map extract. A comparison with the 1857 map shows very little physical change apart from more labourers' cottages being erected on North and South Row. The Toll Bar, which was still collecting tolls in the 1870s, is now the Old Gate House and was occupied by the hind from the nearby Church End Farm. The five pubs and eight water pumps shown are not unusual for communities of this size. (Reproduced from 1897 Ordnance Survey map, 25 inch series, with the kind permission of the Ordnance Survey)

Opposite above: In 1888 Henry Eldon Fletcher, a twenty-two-year-old grocer from Norton, rented the old cottage next to the school on Billingham Green. He converted it to a 'Grocers and Provisions Dealer', known as 'The Billingham Cash Trading Stores'. Selling a wide range of goods, he soon established a successful business both in and beyond Billingham due to his popular delivery service to neighbouring villages and farms. Seen here in around 1894, the shop was attached to premises used by William Atkinson as a joiner's shop. Fletcher later came to live in Billingham and remained there for most of his life.

Opposite below: The village cross, erected in 1893, stood alongside the Norton Road and replaced an old wooden structure. An unsubstantiated story is that it was supposed to have been unveiled by the Prince of Wales as he travelled through the village to Wynyard Hall. However, as nobody had actually informed him about this royal engagement, he continued on his way through the village without stopping – much to the disappointment of the villagers!

By 1902 Henry Eldon Fletcher had bought the cottage and neighbouring barn outright. Here he is with some of his staff outside the shop bearing his name in around 1900. The shop filled a real need in these relatively isolated communities where people would otherwise have had to travel to neighbouring Norton or Stockton – a long journey for many villagers.

This image from around 1899 shows children from the National School with their schoolmaster, George W. Raper. Born in Barnard Castle, Raper was appointed headmaster at the National School in 1898 at the age of thirty-three; he held the post for nearly thirty years. Under his leadership the school was extended and the attendance increased from ninety-eight pupils in 1902 to 222 in 1912. Raper soon became a member of the parish council and played a leading part in village life for many years.

This close-up of the cross looks towards Church View, Settles' grocery and newspaper shop and Church Row, c. 1898. The Settles rented the premises and by 1914 the business and their cottage, situated next to the Black Horse, had been taken over by George Briggs. He greatly extended the business. Delivering newspapers morning and evening meant a walk, twice a day, to Billingham Station to collect newspapers arriving from Middlesbrough, Darlington and Newcastle. Briggs eventually moved to the old blacksmith's premises next to the Smiths Arms; the shop became a cake shop run by Jane Howe. Later in the 1920s it became Poole's Garage, the first garage in the village.

Since Anglo-Saxon times Billingham church has been a local landmark. As well as being a religious institution it was also socially and politically involved in local affairs. The Revd Philip Rudd, the incumbent from 1852 to 1901, exemplified this role by overseeing an extensive rebuilding of the church as well as being closely involved with village life, particularly after the inception of the parish council in 1894. The labourer scything the grass here was Bill Handley, who later died in the First World War. The inset shows Bill and his wife in 1914.

East Row, *c.* 1905. The main building is Brewery House, built in the eighteenth century and known locally as Heslop's Brewery. John Heslop, from Lythe, Yorkshire, was living there in 1861. With his son John he built up a sizeable brewing business owning another brewery in Norton, as well as a number of pubs too. These included, by 1863, the Union Inn (renamed the Station Hotel in around 1866) and later the Black Horse Inn on Billingham Green. However, brewing at Billingham seems to have declined by the early 1900s, probably coinciding with the death of John senior in 1901 at the age of seventy-six. Heslop's Ales continued to be brewed in Norton where John Heslop junior lived. Beyond Brewery House is Wren's farmhouse and the path at the corner of East Row and North Row which went to farm outbuildings used by Fletcher's to store their delivery vehicles.

Opposite above: This view shows Tower House, or 'The Pinnacle', as it was known locally, *c.* 1905. A local story is that George 'Tatie' Robson, who owned the property, was denied planning permission in 1879 to extend the site outwards – so he built upwards! George, originally from Durham, was at various times a grocer, general provisions dealer, potato dealer and farmer. The lychgate constructed from oak in 1883 is visible here, as is the rear of Church View. In the distance are Brewery House and Village Farm.

Opposite below: The Black Horse Hotel, shown here after its extension in around 1904, advertises 'Heslop's Noted Stout' from its window. The newly planted trees have wooden guards around them to prevent them from being damaged by livestock. Purchased from Fewsters in Norton, the trees were part of a scheme of improvements made to Billingham Green in 1904. Six seats and two notice boards were also erected. A group of children have gathered on the school wall, keen to be in the photograph.

Rebecca Golightly was born in 1852 at Grindon. She moved to Cowpen Bewley in around 1871 where she was employed as a farm servant by Joseph Elstob. When he moved to Billingham she became his housekeeper. The relationship obviously flourished as they married in the summer of 1887. Joseph became sub-postmaster at Billingham post office in September 1899, partitioning off a section of their downstairs living room for this purpose. Mrs Elstob delivered the mail on foot around the village, then by bike to the outlying farms and to Wolviston. Joseph was also church caretaker, one of his duties being to walk round each evening ringing the curfew – 8 p.m. in the winter and 9 p.m. in the summer. This image shows Mrs Rebecca Elstob outside the old post office in Church Road in around 1902 just after the end of the Boer War (note the recruiting poster). The little girl with her helped with the deliveries.

Opposite above: The removal of the village pumps after water became more widely available in the village caused a lot of debate at parish council meetings during 1895 and 1896. This pump still remained in 1906 close to Fletcher's new grocery shop. The shop replaced Billingham Cash Trading Stores which had been opened by Henry Eldon Fletcher eighteen years previously. Notice a man in the distance riding a penny farthing past the Ship Inn.

Opposite below: As far back as 1828 there were five public houses around Billingham Green. One, the Black Horse Inn, was bought by John Heslop in 1899. He then bought the two cottages next door which he incorporated as part of the inn. Heslop sold beer from the family brewery at the inn, which was said to be favoured by villagers and brewery workers alike. The only fire-fighting appliance in the village was kept in the Black Horse coach house.

This image from 1906 shows the gable end of the Half Moon Inn, an 'alehouse' where the beer was kept in a barrel close to the bar as there were no cellars. Favoured by commercial and agricultural travellers, it stood between the corner of Church Road and the blacksmiths. In 1901 the licensee was a widow aged seventy named Mary Best, born in Norfolk and previously a proprietor (with her husband) of the Blacksmiths Arms in Hartlepool. Four years later Jane Cummings succeeded but it was a brief tenure as the inn lost its licence to trade in 1908.

A painting of the Salutation Inn – artist and date both unknown. It is from before 1893 however, as it shows the original cottage premises before they were replaced in that year. Elizabeth Hildrey, proprietor since the death of her father in the 1860s, was there for over fifty years. Like the other public houses, the Salutation Inn also had its own clientele – in this case 'travellers and the gentry'. It was certainly popular, as it was enlarged again and rebuilt in the early 1930s.

In the 1890s John Thomas Mountain was a blacksmith and landlord of the Smiths Arms, a public house popular with farm and rail workers. Tragically, he died in 1899 aged only forty-five. This poignant image outside the Smiths Arms seems to have been taken on the day of his funeral. His widow Sarah Jane remarried and continued at the pub until the 1920s. In 1929 the pub was rebuilt by Hartlepool brewers J.W. Camerons on land adjacent to this site.

The fifth of Billingham's pubs in 1900 was the Ship Inn. Like the Half Moon Inn, the Ship Inn was regarded by villagers as an 'alehouse'. The Ship Inn too lost its licence – a year after the Half Moon! The last proprietor was a bachelor named John George Smiddy who combined his role with that of being a railway worker too. His aged parents lived with him, and presumably they either ran or helped in the business.

Thomas Taylor started a fish shop in the building which had been the Half Moon Inn. Joseph Lancaster from Billingham bought the shop just before the First World War. He went on to establish a long-running business and Lancaster's Fish Shop was remembered fondly by customers many years later. This image shows Joseph, his wife Jessie and his mother Annie outside the shop.

2

FARMS AND
OTHER PLACES

Wolviston Grange Farm, Billingham

Wolviston Grange Farm, which once stood just behind the
site of the Swan Hotel today. The farmhouse stands behind
the trees which are just visible.

Station Lane, shown here in around 1904 (and later known as Station Road), was the road linking the village to Billingham Station. Just after the exit from the village there were some terraced houses (built in around 1898) and the eighteenth-century farmhouse known as Low Farm, seen here on the left of the picture. Its tenants in the nineteenth century included the Bamlett family who farmed the 100 acres for over half a century. Village entrepreneur Henry Eldon Fletcher, his wife and their five sons were also tenants for a while whilst their new shop and home on Billingham Green were being built.

Originally called 'Hartville' when it was built in the 1870s, this Victorian mansion was later renamed Billingham Hall. The exact year in which it was built – and for whom – is uncertain. James Groves, one of three owners from Hartlepool who made their money in shipping, was living there in 1881 when he died aged fifty-seven. Sometime between 1891 and 1894 it was bought by a Londoner, C.J. Watson Munro. He had been living in Norton and worked as a secretary to an iron-works company. The Hall was sold to another Hartlepool ship-owner, Captain Jesse Lilley, sometime between 1894 and 1901. Lilley came originally from very humble beginnings. The son of a Lincolnshire shepherd, he was an agricultural labourer at the age of eleven. When he died in the summer of 1907, aged sixty, his wife sold the Hall to Charles Nielsen, the third Hartlepool shipping magnate to own the property. Jesse Lilley and his family are shown here sitting in the grounds of Billingham Hall in around 1904.

The first purpose-built station was erected in Billingham in 1841. This was rebuilt in 1866 by the North Eastern Railway and is shown here, *c.* 1900. It had several name changes including Billingham Junction (1878-1893), Billingham (1893-1926) and Billingham on Tees thereafter. This view looks east with the land belonging to Billingham High Grange Farm in the distance.

This view looks in the other direction. The most noticeable feature is the signal box which is not only smaller but is to the north of the station – directly opposite its current position. A train is due as the signalman is looking down the line through the open window and the crossing is closed across the lane from Billingham to Wolviston. In the distance, a group of women dressed in long Victorian-style coats stand on the platform.

The hostelry on this site dates back to the 1830s when the railway was built. Initially known as the Union Inn, it was renamed the Station Hotel in the 1860s when the station was rebuilt. The hotel was at one time owned by Billingham brewing family the Heslops and eventually was bought by Bass. This image is probably from around 1900 and shows landlord John Pitchford, originally from Rotherham, standing at the door. The horse and cart belong to George Burns, a fish merchant from West Hartlepool.

The area north of the station remained undeveloped until the 1890s when a small number of large detached houses were built. The parish council, in October 1897 and again in July 1898, were asked to have gas lamps erected 'along the road from the station to Sandy Lane end.' Despite its lack of clarity, this image, taken almost a century ago, is an unusual view of 'Greenholme', one of the properties on Wolviston Road. The photograph was taken from across the fields which once lay behind the house. Today these ploughed fields lie beneath housing along Roseberry Road.

This view is the High Street, Wolviston, *c.* 1904. The Red Lion, the King's Arms, the White Swan and the Wellington Inn, four of the five public houses in Wolviston, are visible here. The inset advertises a dance at the King's Arms in 1921. Following its eventual sale in October 1937, the King's Arms licence was transferred to a new establishment south of the village on the site of the former Wolviston Pottery. The licence from the White Swan was also transferred (to the Swan Hotel in Billingham), whilst the Red Lion ceased to trade at all.

St Peter's church, *c.* 1902. Built in 1876, St Peter's replaced an earlier structure in the village. The horse and the hay cart depict an idyllic scene which belies the hard life led by many who farmed the land. Nevertheless, this image reflects a scene of tranquillity from a bygone age.

Wolviston Mill was one of a number of watermills supplied by Billingham Beck and its tributaries. The watermills were part of the local economy for many centuries. Shown here in 1906, it later fell into disuse and was eventually demolished in the 1970s.

Norton Mill (mentioned in the *Boldon Book* in 1183) stood on high ground west of Billingham Bottoms. An ancient pathway went across the Bottoms from the mill to Chapel Road in Billingham. This view dates from 1900 when both Norton and Wolviston Mills were owned by the Watson family. Like Wolviston Mill, Norton Mill also fell into decline and by 1924 was no longer in use. Extensively damaged by a bomb in 1940, the remains of the mill disappeared under the present A19 route when it was built in the 1970s.

Billingham Mill, seen here in a somewhat dilapidated state in around 1900, was demolished so long ago that few people remember it today. There is mention of Billingham Mill as far back as 1368 and 1380 when villagers were told by the Halmote Court that they had to grind their corn there. Although by the seventeenth century there seems to have been some decline in the importance of the mill, it continued to be used by villagers. In fact, some importance seems to have been regained as it was rebuilt between 1700 and 1720. The buildings shown here date from that time.

Local residents recall the rural tranquillity of the area around Billingham Mill, an area which was popular for wildfowling. The road from Billingham, Mill Lane, ended at the mill, a footpath continuing across a bridge over the mill race to Portrack. Known locally as 'Moon's Mill', Billingham Mill was last worked by the Moon family in around 1903-1906. It later became a house for the hind who worked at nearby Brook House Farm. The two men here are standing next to Billingham Beck near to the fork with the mill race. The mill is in the distance. Both the mill and the farm were demolished in the early 1930s as ICI continued to expand.

This view shows Billingham from the west. In the distance Billingham church stands high above the surrounding area. It was taken before Billingham expanded in the 1920s when the area around the church was built upon. Billingham Bank, created by the Turnpike Trust in 1789, is shown before it was widened in the late 1920s. The weir on Billingham Beck is also visible.

Billingham Bottoms was a popular venue for ice skating, attracting crowds from a wide area. In January 1909 nineteen-year-old Gwen Nielsen (later to live in Billingham Hall) wrote in her diary of going 'with a large party from her home [in Hartlepool] to Billingham skating... and [that] the train was 54 minutes late home.' This view from around 1905 shows Billingham church in the distance, flanked by the trees on Billingham Bank whilst smoke or steam is rising from John Robinson's brickworks on Chapel Road.

This image from around 1890 is inconclusively titled 'a farm in Billingham', but evidence from other sources suggests it is Brook House Farm. The 200-acre farm was situated a field away from Billingham Mill. The Robinson family lived at Brook House Farm for over sixty years.

Billingham Grange, a farm of over 200 acres, was on Chilton's Lane (named Marsh Lane until the 1860s). It was farmed for many years by the Chilton family, one of whom sold Middlesbrough Farm in 1828 to the consortium who built the town of Middlesbrough. John Emmet was the last person to farm at Billingham Grange before the land was taken over by the Ministry of Munitions in 1917. The eighteenth-century farmhouse became the first offices of Synthetic Ammonia & Nitrates Ltd and remained part of the factory until 1982 when it was demolished. This view dates from the early 1920s, the inset being a drawing of the farm from around 1882.

Tibbersley Farm, like Billingham Grange, was reached by Chilton's Lane. Smaller than Billingham Grange, the 100 acres also became part of the Synthetic Ammonia & Nitrates Ltd factory. Tibbersley Farm was bordered to the south by the river, and Stockton Races were held on land at the farm for a number of years. The 1901 census shows that in addition to the Forster family, four farm servants lived and worked at the eighteenth-century farm.

John Forster and his wife Elizabeth (seen here in around 1908) moved to Tibbersley Farm from Norton in the early 1890s. John, born in Shildon in around 1848, was an engineer before he moved to Tibbersley Farm. He was there for almost thirty years before the farm was taken over by the Synthetic Ammonia & Nitrates Ltd factory. A respected local figure, John Forster was particularly active in the parish council before the First World War.

STOCKTON RACES.

OVER THE NEW COURSE, AT TIBBERSLY.

THURSDAY, 29th AUGUST, 1839.

STEWARDS,—

THE EARL OF EGLINTON, JOHN BELL, ESQ., JOHN ALLAN, ESQ.

FIRST DAY.—THURSDAY.

THE CLARET STAKES.—A Sweepstakes of 10 sov. each, with 30 sov. added for the second horse, for two year olds. Colts, 8st 3lb; fillies, 8st. The winner to give four dozen of Claret. To start at the Blue Post—Seven furlongs.

Mr Attwood's b c Avicenna
— Attwood's b c by Physician or Leonardo, out of Eliza
— Powlett's b c by Liverpool, out of Miss Fanny's dam
— Wilkin's c c by Satan, out of Abraham Newland's dam
— Wilkin's br c by Satan, dam by Monreith
— Williamson na. br c by Voltaire, out of sis. to Katnuoff
— Bell's b f by Gainsbro, out of Golden Drop's dam
— Orde's b f Queen Bee, by Liverpool, out of Tomboy's dam
— Chilton's b c Neptune, by Physician
Lord Eglinton's br f Devergild, by Liverpool
Mr Jaques's b f Interlude, by Physician
— Smith's b c by Memnon Junior, out of Amulet
— Heseltine's b f sister to slashing Harry
— Bowes's b c by Curtius, out of Gitaide Fairy
— J. O. Farlies's c c Ambassadore, by Plenipotentiary
— Pierse's b c by Physician
— Mr Blakelock's b f Hygeia, by Physician
— Pierse's b c by Voltaire, dam by Comus
— Clarke's b c The Tory, by Paulus

A SWEEPSTAKES of 20 sov each, for three and four years old Mares. Three years old, 7st 5lbs; four, 8st 5lbs, Maiden four years olds allowed 3 lbs. One mile and a half.

The Earl of Eglintone's Opera, 4 y o.
The Duke of Cleveland's Virginia, 4 y o.
Mr Bowes's Mickellou Maid, 3 y o.
— Vansittart's b f by Sandbeck, 3 y o.
— Charles Monk's b f Garland, 4 y o,

THE THIRSK STAKES. A Sweepstakes of 20 sov. each, 10 sov. forfeit, with 20 sov. added by John Bell, Esq., for two year olds. Colts to carry 8st 4lb, fillies,8st. Two year old course. Six furlongs.

Duke of Cleveland's c c by Emilius, out of Farce
Mr Bowes's b c Middleham, by Memnon Jun.
— Kirby's b f by Liverpool, out of Dirmid's dam
— King's bk c by Tomboy
— Dawson na. br c The Young Un, by Satan
— Shepherd's br c Viceroy, by Voltaire

SECOND DAY.—FRIDAY.

A GOLD CUP, value 100 sov by subscription of 10 sov each; the surplus in specie. Three years olds, 6st 7lb; four, 8st; five, 8st 13lb; six and aged 8st 7lb Mares and geldings and maiden horses allowed 3lb. A winner of a cup, value 100 sov ip the present year, to carry 3lb extra. Any four year old, or upwards, that has not won above £50, allowed 7lbs. Twice round.

SUBSCRIBERS—

Mr Vansittart	The Earl of Eglinton
Col. Hildyard	Mr Allan
Mr Bell	Mr Orde
Mr Scurfield	Mr Hutchinson
Mr Bowes	Sir James Boswell

THE LONDONDERRY STAKES.—A Sweepstakes of 10 sov. each, for three year old colts and fillies; colts to carry 8st 4lb, fillies 8st 1lb. One mile and a half.

The Earl of Eglinton's b g Urish
Mr Shafloe's b c by Physician, dam by Whitworth
— Allan na. br f by Voltaire, out of Am ulet
— Attwood's c c by Calisthanes
— Watkin's b f No. 3, by Jerry
— Chilton's b c by Physician, out of Fisher Lass

A HUNTER'S STAKE.—A Sweepstakes of 10 sov. each, with 20 sov. added, for bona fide Hunters. Certificates to be produced if required. Four years old 10st 12lb; five, 11st 7lb; six and aged, 12st; half bred horses allowed 12lb; a winner of £50 at any one time in the present year to carry 3lb. extra. To start at the Blue Post—about two miles. Gentlemen riders. The winner to give £10 towards the new race course.

THE CLEVELAND STAKE, of 20 sov each, for two year old colts and fillies. Colts 8st 4lbs; fillies 8st. 1lb. To start at the Red Post—rather more than half a mile.

Lord Londonderry's br f Venus de Medici, by Voltaire
The Duke of Cleveland's b f by Physician, out of Matilda
Mr Bowes's b c by Memnon, Jun., out of Henrietta
— Parkin's b c Broadwith, by Liverpool
— Simpson's br f Light Saddle, by the Saddler

THIRD DAY.—SATURDAY.

THE ALL AGED STAKE of 10 sov. each, with 25 sov. added by John Bowes, Esq., M. P. Three years old, 7st; four, 8st 5lb; five, 8st 12lb: six and aged, 9st 2lb. Mares and Geldings allowed 3lb, and Maiden horses at the time of starting allowed 5lb. The winner to be sold for 300 sov. if demanded. To start at the Blue Post—about two miles. The owner of the second horse to receive £10 out of the stake.

Mr Vansittart's b f by Sandbeck, out of Darlolita, 3y.
Mr Sutton na. Sweet Jessy, by Jerry, 3y.
Mr Allan na. br f by Voltaire, out of Amulet, 3y.
Mr King's b f Livy, by Langar, 3y.
Mr Loy's b c Arrorat, by Liverpool, out of White Rose by Comus, 3y.

THE MIDDLESBRO' STAKE, a sweepstake of 10 sov each, p. p. with 20 sov. added by the inhabitants of Middlesbro', The second horse to receive £10 out of the Stake. Two years old to carry 6st 7lb; three 8st 10lb. four 9st 4lb; five 9st 9lb; six and aged 9st 13lb. Mares and geldings allowed 3lb. To start at the first turn—about one Mile.

THE MARINERS' STAKE.—A Sweepstakes of 3 sov. each, with 20 sov. added by the Captains of the Tees and their friends, for horses used solely for Agricultural purposes, and to be ridden by Captains of Ships. The second horse to save his Stake. Heats—once round. The horses to be handicapped by the Clerk of the Course, or who he may appoint, opposite the Stand on the race course, at ten o'clock in the morning of the race.

The Cup, the Hunters' Stake, the Middlesbro' Stake, and the Mariner's Stake, all to close and name to the Clerk of the Course, Stockton, on or before 7 o'clock on Saturday evening, the 24th of August.

JOHN JACKSON, CLERK OF THE COURSE.

Any person wishing to obtain a correct list of the full entry or these races, may do so by applying at the office of the printer, after 8 o'clock on Monday morning, the 26th.

☞ Mr Jackson has carried out a Quay on the race course to low water, so that Steam Boats may land passengers at any part of the tide, with the greatest comfort and safety.

J. PROCTER, PRINTER, HARTLEPOOL.

Racing at Stockton began in 1724 at Mandale Carrs (now part of the University at Stockton) and continued there until the meetings lapsed in 1816. In 1825 the meetings were revived and held at Tibbersley Farm, Billingham. Racing was usually held over two or three days. Rules for spectators included 'no riding on that part of the course where the horses run', the stipulation that loose dogs would be shot and the request that 'three pence should be contributed towards costs' whilst no additional charge would be made for use of the 'gangway'. This was a landing stage at the course where parties disembarked on arrival by the river, from Stockton and elsewhere. From the landing stage they walked across the fields to the course and the betting ring just in front of the farmhouse. This remarkable artefact is a racecard from a meeting in 1839 held from 29 to 31 August. John Jackson, who then farmed at Tibbersley, was clerk of the course. A light-hearted diversion on the last day was the 'Mariners' Stakes', a race for farm horses to be ridden only by captains of ships. On the death of Jackson in 1845 the races again lapsed. Racing began again in 1855 on a course at Mandale Bottoms, where it continued until the 1980s before being replaced by the Teesside Park development. An attempt in 1881 to revive Billingham Races lasted only for one year.

The Belasis family acquired the land around Belasis Hall at the time of the Norman Conquest. Belasis Hall was a substantial building surrounded by a moat and commanding views across the Tees. Surtees described how John de Belasis, wishing to join one of the Crusades in around 1272, exchanged this manor for cash and a smaller estate at Henknowle, near Bishop Auckland, a move he later regretted. The land subsequently belonged to the Lambton and then the Eden families. The ancient manor house is shown here in around 1935 when it was a farmhouse. It was later bombed during the Second World War.

Billingham was linked to Cowpen Bewley by Cowpen Lane, a long and isolated road. This image, taken just beyond Cowpen Gate, shows Cowpen Lane in the early 1900s. The lane is in a very poor state of repair but is typical of many local rural roads at this time.

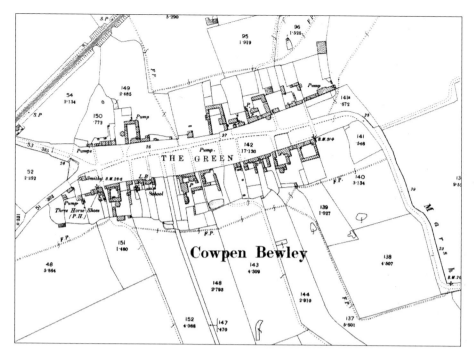

This map of Cowpen Bewley in 1897 shows a pattern of housing which dates back to Norman England. The two rows of properties adjoining the village green with fields behind are typical of the way the Normans planned their settlements. A more recent building, the school, which opened in 1874, is also visible, as is the village pond and the Three Horse Shoes, a long established public house. Several water pumps can also be seen on the map. (Reproduced from 1897 Ordnance Survey map, 25 inch series, with the kind permission of the Ordnance Survey)

The village of Cowpen Bewley was once part of the estate of Beaulieu, a nearby moated house owned by Durham Priory. Although the houses visible in this image from around 1906 are post seventeenth-century, the pattern of housing in the village has changed little since medieval times. The village had several farms whilst a road to Haverton Hill, completed just before the First World War, was an important link to local industrial development.

This illustration is from *A History of Coal, Coke, Coalfields and Iron Manufacture in Northern England*, first published in 1860. Originally the Stockton and Darlington Railway intended to use Haverton Hill as a shipping point for coal, but abandoned this in favour of using Middlesbrough. When the Clarence Railway took over the scheme they extended the line to Samphire Batts – renamed Port Clarence, a point where deep water allowed access for shipping. The coal drops are shown operating in this drawing which is dated 1841.

3

LIFE AT BILLINGHAM HALL

Gwen Nielsen lived at Billingham Hall between 1909 and 1919 and kept a detailed record of her life there, much of which has been used to provide information for this chapter. Gwen was typical of her time, living at home and enjoying a life which embraced a variety of social functions. During the First World War Gwen became a VAD nurse, being stationed at the Army Hospital, Dinsdale. Towards the end of the war Gwen became engaged to Hugh Allport Hay and they went on to marry in 1919. This image from April 1917 shows Gwen and Hugh in a snowy driveway at Billingham Hall.

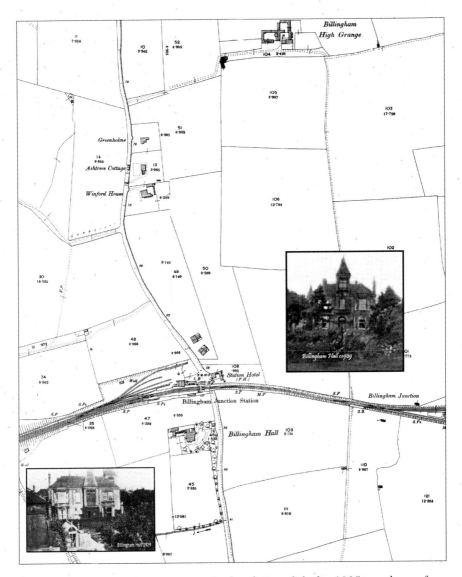

Billingham Hall is Billingham's forgotten landmark. Demolished in 1935 to make way for a housing development, very few people alive today recall the building. However, a collection of images have recently been made available by the Nielsen family, owners of the Hall between 1909 and 1922. These images, never before published, have been digitally restored to show something of life at Billingham Hall at that time. Built in the early 1870s, three families lived at Billingham Hall before Hartlepool shipowner Charles Nielsen and his wife Margaret, with their two children, moved there on 16 April 1909. It is mainly due to the photographic work and daily diary kept by daughter Gwen at the age of twenty that a record of life at Billingham Hall has been preserved. An impressive building, Billingham Hall was part of a 1.5 acre site and was reached by a driveway from the Wolviston Road. A belt of tall poplar trees stood in the grounds ensuring privacy for the residents. This 1897 map extract shows the grounds as well as the general location of the Hall. The two insets show the south aspect of the Hall in 1909 and the west aspect in 1929. (Reproduced from 1897 Ordnance Survey map, 25 inch series, with the kind permission of the Ordnance Survey)

This view from May 1910 looks east with the south aspect of the house visible. Villagers recalled the gardens as being impressive with urns of flowers surrounding the house, one of which can be seen here. Although a number of servants (including a gardener) were employed at the Hall, daughter Gwen writes of many enjoyable family afternoons working in the garden. The trees along the road to Wolviston are in the background.

This image, dated 14 March 1915, shows the driveway which swept around the house from the road. The Nielsen family were one of the few in Billingham with a car before the First World War so this driveway was in regular use. The south-east corner of the house is to the right of the picture. Behind the trees is a 3.5-acre field farmed by the Dixons who lived in the village at Glebe Farm.

During the Nielsens' first summer in Billingham, Whitsuntide seems to have been a time of relaxation and an opportunity for a number of photographs to be taken of their new home. Charles Luis (known as Luis), who was aged eight when the family moved to the Hall, is seen here on 1 June 1909 with his father Charles outside the main entrance to the Hall. The previous day, Whit Monday, had seen a family gathering at the Hall with a dinner being held there in the evening. Luis later became a pupil at Aysgarth School so he spent term times away from the Hall.

This is a second image taken on 1 June 1909. Luis is in the gardens at Billingham Hall, with the west prospect of the Hall behind him. Despite a cool showery spring in 1909, Gwen writes of many days spent out in the garden. Evenings were often spent entertaining friends, playing billiards or listening to the gramophone. On other occasions the family enjoyed country walks or cycle rides along Sandy Lane or the road to Wolviston.

This image was taken at the south-facing main entrance into the Hall. Gwen can be seen with her Uncle Charles, who visited the Hall with his wife Addie, over Whitsuntide. In the background is a distant hedgerow behind which lay open farmland stretching across to Norton.

There are very few images which show the interior of Billingham Hall. Consequently this image has been included despite its poor quality – even after some restoration. Taken in the drawing room that looked south across the gardens to the village of Billingham, it shows Hans Nielsen, the elder brother of Charles, with two relatives visiting from Denmark. Jens Christian Nielsen, Gwen's grandfather, moved to England from Denmark in 1846 where he established a successful shipping company. Although he was naturalised as a British subject in 1856, he retained close contact with his relatives in Denmark.

On Thursday 1 June 1911 Charles and Margaret Nielsen celebrated their twenty-fifth wedding anniversary. A large family gathering had assembled by tea-time of the previous day and were all staying at the Hall. The celebrations included a garden party in the grounds of Billingham Hall during the day followed in the evening by a dinner party for eighteen people. Some of the family stayed on for a few days and these two delightful images were taken on Saturday evening, 3 June 1911. Gwen, seen here on the right, describes this as being a 'gramophone party', and indeed the gramophone can be seen on a table outside the front door. The other girls are two cousins who were also staying at the Hall.

This enchanting image from the same evening is entitled 'Dancing with Sylvia' and is a splendid picture of two young women having fun nearly a century ago. Sylvia and her parents stayed on at the Hall for nearly two weeks after the silver wedding celebrations, going for days out and visiting other relatives.

Another rare image taken inside shows Sylvia in the drawing room at Billingham Hall. Freda Bell, from nearby Billingham High Grange, occasionally visited the Hall and described it as 'a beautiful place with a lovely stained-glass window. There was a lounge and dining room on either side of the front entrance as you went in. Then there was a drawing room, a morning room, library and kitchens.' Upstairs there was a dressing room and seven bedrooms. These included the East Room – with its magnificent view of the sea and the Tees Bay – the White Room and the Tower Room.

These images were taken on the 12 June 1914 and are again outside the main entrance facing south. The much admired stained-glass window can just be seen in both images. On the left is Charles Nielsen with Frank (surname not given) whilst the other image is of Gwen Nielsen. This seems to have been a very carefree time in Gwen's life, with a constant social whirl of tennis tournaments, visits to the theatre, meeting friends for tea, shopping and local dances.

Tennis was a popular activity at Billingham Hall and tennis parties were often held both there and at other country houses in the area. This image is entitled 'The tennis crowd at Billingham Hall 1911' and includes Gwen, second right, next to her Uncle Hans. Her brother, Luis, is also in the picture – he is aged eleven here.

Gwen woke at 8.15 a.m. on Wednesday 16 December 1914 to the sound of bombing over Hartlepool. With her mother she tried to visit there later that day only to be stopped at Wolviston. She writes of meeting people walking along the Wolviston Road looking for shelter, having abandoned Hartlepool due to fear of another attack. Two days later on the Friday, after a further scare that morning, they finally saw for themselves the extensive damage to the town. Nevertheless, normal life continued wherever possible. Gwen and Luis are shown here preparing the tennis courts at the Hall in 1916. Within a short time Luis joined the Officer Training Corps and Gwen, already training to be a VAD, went away to work in a military hospital.

Hugh Allport Hay, from Wiltshire, occasionally visited Billingham Hall whilst a student at Durham University before he graduated in 1910. The Hay family had local connections as his father was born in Sunderland and his aunt, Elfleda, lived in Norton having married Hans Nielsen, Gwen's uncle. Hugh continued to visit during the war and is shown here on the left of the group. A Mr Bennett is in the middle, whilst on the right is Hugh's younger brother Roger Bolton Hay, clearly struggling to get the dog to face the camera! The image is dated 4 July 1915.

Hugh joined the West Yorkshire Regiment at the start of war in 1914 whilst Roger, about to go up to Oxford, joined the Universities and Public Schools Battalion. In 1915 he also joined the West Yorks. Both became lieutenants seconded to the Royal Flying Corps and remarkably both were also awarded the Military Cross, Hugh in 1916 and Roger in June 1917. However, on 17 July 1917, Roger was shot whilst on a reconnaissance flight over the front line. He was posted as missing, but having been captured, he died later that day from his wounds. It was not until 25 August 1917 that Gwen recorded in her diary that his parents had received news of his death. He was aged twenty-two and was buried in a cemetery in Ostend.

A very sunny Whitsuntide ended with a family gathering on Friday 28 May 1915. Gwen's cousin Vera Guthe came for tea with her husband Tom and their two daughters. Tom, seen here holding Ithiel, aged four, and Beryl, two, died in France on 13 January 1916 aged thirty-three – his wife Vera was a widow for forty years until her death in 1956. Next to Tom is Roger Hay, waiting to go to the front line with the R.F.C., and Luis, now aged fifteen. Behind Roger is Gwen, now twenty-six. At the back are the two Nielsen brothers, Hans and Charles with Charles' wife Margaret. Vera Guthe is at the front. The image was taken on the south lawn in front of the lounge.

This is Ithiel and Beryl on the lawns on the same day as the previous image. Beryl lived on until 1978 but Ithiel died in 1933 aged only twenty-two.

On 17 September 1916 Gwen was sent to nurse wounded soldiers from the front, at the Army Hospital in Dinsdale. Gwen writes about many of the patients they received, the long shifts on the wards under the vigilant eye of the sister and the camaraderie she found in her work. Look behind Gwen in this image to see the magnificent stained-glass window that was in the main entrance to the Hall. The other image shows sixteen-year-old Luis at the foot of the Hall steps in his OTC uniform.

Winter at Billingham Hall

Easter Monday 1917 was very cold and Gwen writes of heavy snow on several days that week. These two images, both taken near to the main entrance of the Hall, show the gardens and the driveway thick with snow. Luis is throwing the snowball at his sister who was home on leave for a couple of days. By now, almost every week, Gwen recorded either the death or the wounding of family members or close friends in the war.

By 1917 romance had blossomed between Gwen and Hugh. This image was taken by the main entrance in the autumn of that year. The room behind is the dining room. Hugh was home on leave after the death of his brother. Gwen writes that Zeppelin alerts were common and that from Billingham Hall she could see the Zeppelins over the works at Cargo Fleet. On 1 April 1916 she had mentioned a Zeppelin raid during the night at Bell's Iron Works at Port Clarence (several Zeppelin raids took place over the North East in 1916 and 1917).

Another image of Gwen and Hugh with the main entrance to the Hall behind. They are standing on the pathway which went around the Hall. Behind are the two stone lions which stood guarding the steps up to the entrance together with one of the stone urns that marked the corner of the lawn. The gardens at the Hall are remembered well by local residents, in particular the annual display of snowdrops along the tree-lined driveway.

Right: Hugh and Gwen married on 17 September 1919. The wedding, attended by more than 100 guests, was held at Norton parish church, followed by a reception back at Billingham Hall. Here Gwen's Uncle Charles and Uncle Hans pose with her cousin Vera in the grounds of the Hall. A glimpse of the lounge can just be seen behind them.

Below: This image of bridesmaid Nancy Brown (friend of Gwen) from Norton and train-bearer Ithiel Guthe is taken in the gardens at Billingham Hall. The four bridesmaids wore gowns of yellow Georgette with crossover bodices, the skirts being composed entirely of small frills. The two train-bearers wore a frilled yellow georgette frock and carried a silver purse. The flowers were bouquets of yellow chrysanthemums tied with heliotrope ribbon.

The ceremony was performed by Hugh's father, the Revd Reynold Wreford Hay, and the bride was given away by her father Charles Nielsen. Hugh's younger brother Guy was best man. Gwen wore a gown of ivory charmeuse with a full court train of silk net edged with Brussels lace. Her only jewellery was a diamond and aquamarine brooch which, together with a bouquet of white flowers, was a gift from the bridegroom. Here they pose outside the steps of the Hall's entrance.

Taken a moment later, this image gives a full view of the court train. The wedding was the first major post-war social occasion held at Billingham Hall. Nearly twenty guests stayed two days at the Hall, with a special dinner party held on the eve of the wedding. Another dinner party for thirty-one guests was held the following day after the wedding.

Above: This wedding group shows the bride and groom, the best man Guy Hay and the four bridesmaids, Nancy Brown, Gwen's cousin Jane Fernandes and Hugh's two sisters, Isabel and Ethel (Moonie) Hay. Also shown are Ithiel and Beryl Guthe, the two train-bearers. This must have been a very happy occasion tinged with sadness as the guests remembered missing friends and family. The inset is a newspaper report of the wedding.

Right: The happy couple went off in the late afternoon to the south of England for their honeymoon. They were away for several weeks, visiting Harrogate, London and Eastbourne. They also went to visit some of Hugh's family in Lancashire. Here the guests stand around the steps of the Hall's main entrance waiting for the couple to take their leave.

Gwen and Hugh leave Billingham Hall. Most of the honeymoon was spent at the Cavendish Hotel in Eastbourne where they enjoyed some pleasant autumn weather. When they returned they set up home at Richmond House in Stockton. They were to remain there for the whole of their marriage, which lasted for forty-six years until Hugh's death in October 1965.

It is strange to think that not only are the couple in this image no longer with us but that Billingham Hall also is no more. On this day in September 1919 this wedding was a major event in the village and attracted a lot of local attention. The view is a lovely memory of the wedding and stands as an indicator of the slow return to some sort of normality after the terrible events of the First World War. It also allows us to have a full view of the couple including Gwen's wedding dress and the house behind them. It is just possible to see someone looking out from the house, obviously wanting to see the photographer at work. Now nearly a century later we look at events very definitely of another age.

4

GREEN FIELDS NO MORE

View from Furness Shipyard towards Chilton's Lane c1928

Industrial development before the First World War had been confined mainly to the area east of Billingham, with a number of salt works, iron works, as well as a cement works being the main employers. The war became a catalyst for industrial development on a larger scale, which would take over land close to the old village of Billingham. This image shows the industrial sites of the two main employers in this post-war period, Furness Shipbuilding Co. and ICI. The shipyards can be seen in the foreground whilst the site of ICI straddles the old Chilton's Lane.

25-3-19

The development of industry north of the Tees occurred east of Billingham. Haverton Hill and Port Clarence became larger communities compared to Billingham, still a village. Haverton Hill developed after 1830 when a number of small-scale enterprises including a glass works, iron foundry and forge became established. The discovery in 1862 of a salt bed led to several salt works opening, including Tees Salt Works. Other industry included the Pioneer Cement Works and Haverton Hill Brickworks. A significant factor in the growth of Port Clarence was the opening of the Bell Iron Works in 1854.

In 1917 the need to replace ships sunk during the war led to the building of the Furness shipyards at Haverton Hill. The site chosen was a deep-water point on the bend of the river. Despite the 85-acre site being low-lying swamp in need of considerable work, the keel of the first ship was laid in May 1918 and the first ship launched a year later. This image from 25 March 1919 shows a steam crane at work in the construction of the yard. In the distance, St John's church and the adjacent vicarage can be seen.

A major part of the construction was the fitting-out basin shown here. This image, dated 22 July 1919, is evidence of the scale of the work that was involved.

This view looks downriver towards the Transporter Bridge. In the foreground, construction of the yard is ongoing. Across the river from the shipyard was the Ironmasters' District, an area of iron and steel works that stretched along the Tees from Newport to the old town of Middlesbrough. A slag heap can be seen in the distance.

With such an increasing population there was an urgent need for new housing. The Furness Estate, shown here under construction on 20 May 1919, was built on an area close to the ancient Belasis Hall and Middle Belasis Farm. Consisting of 564 houses, this estate was known as 'Belasis Garden City'. Like those later to be built at Billingham, the houses were of a high quality and the development was regarded as a model of its kind.

The Furness Offices, shown here in the 1920s, stood at the entrance of the yard. The impressive building was indicative of the status that the shipyard enjoyed at this time.

In 1917 the Ministry of Munitions, after consultations with Brunner Mond, chose a site east of Billingham village for a new nitrates factory. Factors behind this choice included the availability of raw materials, a local labour force, a basic transport infrastructure and, most important, electricity from the Newcastle Electric Co.'s new power station nearby. Construction at Billingham began in 1918, only to be halted when the First World War ended later that year and the need for explosives became less important. Chilton's Lane, which ran through the middle of the proposed factory site, is shown here as not much more than a cart track.

When the Ministry of Munitions halted construction of the factory it was advertised for sale in *The Times* in November 1919. In April 1920 the same newspaper carried an article confirming the sale to Brunner Mond to be developed as a subsidiary company, Synthetic Ammonia and Nitrates Ltd. The production of ammonia nitrates and other by-products would be their eventual aim, but a great deal of development was first necessary. The farmhouse at Billingham Grange (used as offices by the Ministry of Munitions' constructors) is shown here – the insets are the Nitrogen Products Committee Report and the sale advert in *The Times*, both from 1919.

Amos Cowap famously called the site 'a good imitation of a prairie', and guests were invited along for the rough shooting. This image is taken close to the farmhouse and Cowap's description can be verified. D. L. White, who is shown here, was employed by the Ministry in 1918. He remained until 1935 when he retired as cashier for ICI Billingham. The inset shows one of the partly built gas holders which stood alongside an ash path close to the farmhouse.

Opposite above: An Executive Committee was established in November 1920 with George Pollitt as chief executive. He became a major force in the Billingham project, urging that 'housing, laboratory, new road, railway access... be hurried forward'. By early 1921 contracts for housing in Mill Lane and the Roscoe Road/Crescent Avenue area were issued and work on the plant had also started. However, in May 1921 Brunner cut their financial support because of industrial unrest and trade depression. The Billingham project was kept alive on a minimum budget by Pollitt but with major changes, including the committee having to be content with plans for a temporary 'scratch plant'. The Grange, seen here in the summer of 1921, was the main office for seven years. In this view from the front garden, complete with fruit trees, in the summer of 1921, an employee can be seen walking from the wooden huts, which acted as administration offices, along to the farmhouse.

Opposite below: The men leading the development at Billingham were based here at the Grange farmhouse; George Pollitt was downstairs on the left, Amos Cowap on the right, whilst Herbert Humphrey and Philip Dickens were both upstairs. Chemist Dr Roland Slade, awaiting a laboratory, had a small room at the back of the house. Philip Dickens had the Grange kitchen as his secretarial office!

Billingham Grange site 1

The Ministry of Munitions' site contained some permanent buildings (workshops and stores), a number of half-built foundations, some temporary wooden buildings and the old farm buildings. This multi-view shows an example of these in the winter and summer of 1922 along with some of the personnel who worked in them. Working here in this rural area must have brought its own challenges and it is a tribute to those employed in the early days that these were met in such a positive and enterprising way.

Opposite above: This remarkable aerial view show the factory in its early days, looking across the Grange site towards Tibbersley Farm and Newport in the distance, *c.* 1924. Chilton's Lane is mid-picture and just behind Tibbersley Farm is a short stretch of an unfinished road which later became New Road. The site where Cassel Works would later be built is still fields and hedgerows.

Opposite below: Taken from a glass negative, the clarity of this image of the construction of the Synthetic Ammonia & Nitrates Ltd factory is remarkable. Many of these views have never been published before and they provide a unique record of these pioneer days when the juxtaposition of industry and agriculture was so evident. This wonderful aerial view shows the site late in 1923. Number one is a view towards the gas plant from the water cooling pool; number two, the sulphate silo; number three, the sulphate plant; number four, the ammonia plant; number five, the stores; number six, the purge gas holder; numbers seven and eight, the boiler plants and number nine, the workshops.

Middlesbrough — Newport — R. Tees — Billingham Beck — Tibbersley Farm — Chilton's Lane — Billingham Grange — Haverton Hill — Belasis Halt — Billingham

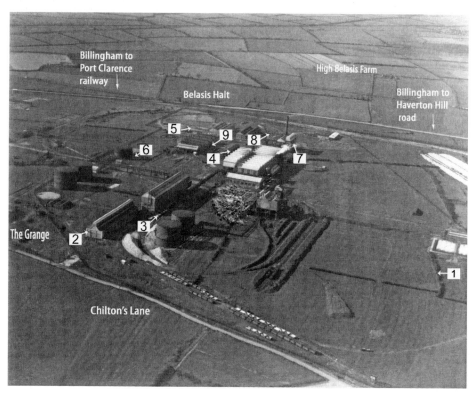

Billingham to Port Clarence railway — High Belasis Farm — Belasis Halt — Billingham to Haverton Hill road — The Grange — Chilton's Lane

5 9 8 6 4 7 3 2 1

A view to the gas plant from the water cooling pool. The site is in its early days of construction here with the sulphate plant visible but only half built.

Railway lines were built to move materials around on site. The site was linked with the LNER Haverton Hill to Billingham railway line to bring in construction materials. The use of the railways can be seen in this image, from late 1922, showing the construction of the sulphate silo in the foreground and the sulphate plant in the distance. The catalysed gas holder can also be seen. Steam rising from the crane on the left and men working on the steel framework of the silo are also visible.

This multi-view shows a close up of the construction of the sulphate plant (top left) and the framework for the ammonia plant (top right). The stores (bottom left) which stood close to the Billingham to Haverton Hill Railway are shown when complete as men unload materials from a rail wagon. This image is taken from the end of the workshops shown in the next image (bottom right) which is taken from the western perimeter of the site at this time, probably December 1922.

These images show the construction of the boiler plant with each image being taken from different viewpoints. The boiler plant was providing steam from mid-1923.

This image looks west from the edge of the Grange towards Billingham, *c.* 1923. In the foreground are the workshops with the purge gas holder behind them. Beyond this point the site is still mostly undeveloped, with only a few huts in place at this stage.

Research was crucial to development. Plans for three blocks of laboratories were passed in March 1921 and they were operational in 1922. Dr Kenneth Warne, who began work in the new Research Buildings in January 1922 as a laboratory boy, recalls that 'they were built about half a mile away from the Grange, standing back from Chilton's Lane behind a large meadow which, during the summer, became a blaze of poppies and marguerites.' The meadow, visible here, later became the site of the first main Synthetic Ammonia & Nitrates Ltd offices.

One of the early laboratories where Dr Warne worked is shown here and the insets show some images of the men who worked there in 1922. The original scratch plant was renamed No. 2 Unit (No. 1 Unit was an experimental unit in Runcorn), but plans to be operational in January 1923 were halted by further labour problems. However, Pollitt was undeterred, and on Christmas Eve 1923 Dr Roland Slade reported to the Executive Committee that the 'first traces of ammonia had appeared at 11.30 p.m. on December 22nd.'

This is a view from the roof of the Research Buildings looking east down Chilton's Lane towards Billingham Grange. It is another example of an image restored from a glass negative and is again remarkable for showing the way in which agriculture was rapidly giving way to industry. The factory can be seen in the distance whilst in the foreground are hedgerows, a haystack and a field in which the strips from medieval farming are still to be seen.

The location of this image, again taken from a glass negative, is uncertain despite considerable restoration. What can be established is that it is looking towards the Ironmasters' District south of the River Tees. The silhouette of a farmhouse can be seen in the middle distance. Obviously a road is being constructed – possibly New Road? However, the foreground seems to show fencing and a pathway belonging to a house, so is it perhaps the construction of Mill Lane, with Brook House Farm in the background, seen from South View in the village?

This is the new housing at the end of Mill Lane in July 1922. Farmland is on the right and the fencing around the new factory site is visible behind the houses. In the distance are the chimneys of Middlesbrough and Brook House Farm.

The new company wanted to close Chilton's Lane, which ran through the middle of their site, but to do so they were required to build an alternative road. New Road was first proposed in 1920 but obtaining the necessary permissions was a lengthy process and with company expenditure restricted in the early 1920s, it was 1924 before the construction of the road got underway in earnest. The road was finally opened on 30 March 1925 and Chilton's Lane was closed, an event which V.E. Parkes said was for many 'the overt and decisive step from a country site to an industrial area.'

This aerial view shows the site in 1924 looking west from close to the river. It gives a fine overall view of the site at a time when the first phase of development, i.e. the running of the No. 2 Unit, had come to fruition. In the top left of the image old Cowpen Lane is visible, as is Cowpen Gate crossing. This area of farmland, very isolated at this time, would soon disappear as the Cowpen Lane housing estate was built here in the early 1930s.

This image also shows the factory following the construction of the first phase of development. The Grange is in the foreground on Chilton's Lane and the view looks to the north to the road from Haverton Hill to Billingham. The factory in this early stage is clearly visible with the original ash path still to be seen going behind the farm and past the gas holders. There is little development yet to the south of Chilton's Lane, which is still open as a public road. By July 1925 600 workers were engaged in the production of ammonium sulphate.

This aerial image from the early 1920s is a perfect way to end this chapter as it captures not only the building of the Synthonia Ammonia and Nitrates factory but looks in the distance towards the already established Furness Shipyard. The full extent of the development of Haverton Hill can also be appreciated as well as the other industry in the area.

5

GROWING UP

South View & Belasis Lane

The coming of industry on a large scale brought many changes to the village of Billingham. Previously centred on Billingham Green, a new community now grew up away from this area with major housing and commercial developments changing the face of Billingham forever. This image encapsulates the old and the new; showing on the left 'Seven Steps', one of the old cottages on South View, whilst in the distance is the new Co-operative Stores, then Billingham's premier shopping experience.

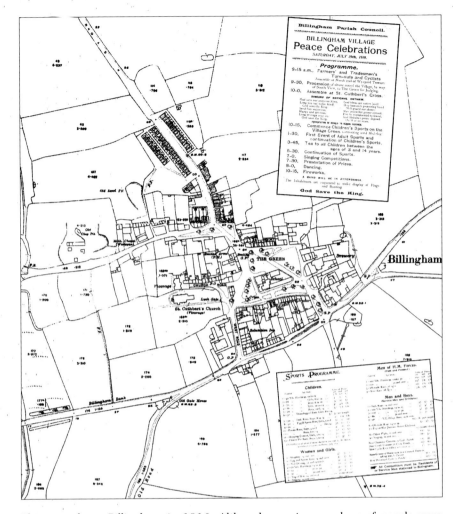

This map shows Billingham in 1916. Although growing numbers of people were employed in the new factories at Haverton Hill and Port Clarence, the village of Billingham remained largely unaltered – a state of affairs which would soon change considerably. As plots around Billingham Green were built on, more available land was sought. Some building occurred along Chapel Road, and there were small developments close to Low Farm as well as at the corner of Station Lane and Parklands Avenue. The first significant development was the building of approximately fifty houses between 1900 and 1905, when Wilson Terrace (now part of Station Road), Wynyard Terrace, opposite, and Stockton Street were built. This new housing along Station Road can be seen on the map. The growth of Billingham in the 1920s led to the old parish council being replaced in 1922 by an Urban District Council and this new body oversaw vigorous social and economic growth. One of the last events to be held in the old village was the Peace Celebrations held on 19 July 1919. With a procession, religious service, sports, a free tea and evening entertainment, this event, with hindsight, can be regarded as the end of an era. Old Billingham village, a self-contained ancient community, was changing quickly. The new Billingham would expand beyond all expectations and become known far and wide. (Reproduced from 1916 Ordnance Survey map, 25 inch series, with the kind permission of the Ordnance Survey)

In 1917 the Newcastle Electric Supply Co. who were building the North Tees Power Station on the north bank of the Tees, built their 'Garden City'. A small estate of seventy-three houses built close to Old Road at the top of Billingham Bank, it housed approximately 300 people. The views here show West Avenue under construction, and when it was completed. By 1922 Synthetic Ammonia & Nitrates Ltd were also building houses for their employees, among them houses at Roscoe Road shown here in the bottom right image.

This view looks northwards towards South View and Belasis Lane. The end of Town End Farm and a Blumer's bus are also visible. There had been a pond at the junction of Belasis Lane and Mill Lane as far back as 1775 but by the 1920s it had become a 'stinking mess in need of great attention'. The council, in an attempt to rectify this, created a park with a shrubbery and a paddling pool and this can be seen in the foreground.

The rapid expansion of Synthetic Ammonia & Nitrates Ltd was the driving force behind the growth of Billingham. All around Billingham Green, the old roads were improved and new ones were built as the desperate need for housing was addressed. The first housing developments from 1922-1925 were close to the factory in Mill Lane, Roscoe Road and Crescent Road. By 1927 more housing had been erected in Imperial Road, Mond Crescent, Brunner Road and New Road. The main image shows Mill Lane. In the distance Town End Farm has been demolished; the site would soon become the new Co-operative Stores building.

The northern end of Mill Lane and Billingham Picture House, together with the park, are all seen in this view, c. 1929. Billingham Urban District Council minutes for 1927-1928 reflect the growth around Mill Lane with a large number of plans for commercial development being approved. In 1928 a 'fine new shopping centre [was]... being built to cope with the demands of an ever growing population' and by December 1928 it was reported that 'between twenty to thirty brightly decorated shop windows stood where... there was not a single establishment six months ago'.

Plans for a cinema to be built on the corner of Mill Lane and South View were approved in February 1928. The Billingham Picture House, costing £10,000 and accommodating 700 people, was opened on 8 October 1928. The managing director was Mr R.S. Groves of Eaglescliffe and the programme for the grand opening was the popular comedy *The Kid Brother* with Harold Lloyd, followed by a performance of the Synthetic Male Voice Choir. This image is from 1935, when the main feature was Shirley Temple starring in *Our Little Girl*. The insets are from a programme card for January 1938.

In May 1930 a new Co-operative Stores building was opened on the site of Town End Farm. It was the thirtieth shop of the Stockton Society with a shop frontage of 270ft and was a prototype of today's shopping centres with eight different shops ranging from a butcher's to a barber's shop. It also had a public hall seating 650 people. The inset is a cover from the programme for a 'Record Recital' in November 1930. Local bands like the Venus Dance Band played here regularly.

This view of Billingham Green looks east from outside the church towards the Church of England school which stood close to Fletcher's shop. By 1926 the rapid population growth meant there was a need for more school places. Plans were passed in 1927 for a school in Belasis Lane and this opened in 1930 as Billingham Intermediate School. Meanwhile, a new Church of England infant school opened in June 1929 in Chapel Road.

This view complements the previous image as it looks towards the church with the houses on the south side of the green being visible, as well as the school. A solitary car is parked outside the Black Horse and a woman, unconcerned about traffic, wheels her pram down the road.

Turning north from the point at which the previous image was taken would give you this view of the road which divided Billingham Green. North Row is on the right whilst in the distance a car is parked outside Cooper's shop located in the former Ship Inn building. On the left is the school. The insets are from the programme of celebrations for the Coronation in 1935.

Tower House (or The Pinnacle) had caused much debate when it was first extended by its owner George Robson. By May 1939 its future was a matter for conjecture as owners Cohen, Jackson and Scott, local solicitors, had ceased to use it. The 60ft high building was pronounced quite sound but when it was put up for either let or sale, there were calls for it to be demolished on the grounds that it was unsightly and obstructed the view of the church.

When this view of Billingham Green in 1927 is compared with similar views from before the First World War, it is evident just how busy the village has become. This image is from outside the Smith's Arms looking south-east to the village school and to Town End Farm. Brewery House still dominates East Row. At this time the house had a kitchen, two large sitting rooms and four very large bedrooms. One of Fletcher's delivery vans can also be seen standing next to the shop.

This view was also taken in around 1927 looking north across Billingham Green towards Chapel Road and Station Road. It shows the Smith's Arms just prior to being rebuilt. Plans from Messrs J.W. Cameron and Co. Ltd were approved in March 1929. A delivery van waits outside Cooper's Grocery Shop which, along with the rest of North Row, was demolished in the 1960s.

This view shows the Half Moon Inn after it had ceased trading in 1908. It became a fish shop, selling fried fish in the premises of the old inn and wet fish in the small cottage next door – seen here behind the bus shelter. This view also shows the premises of the village blacksmith. Local lads like Harry Briggs, the son of George Briggs who took over Settle's newsagents, would often help out in the smithy.

Fletcher's shop, shown here in the 1920s, must have thrived with the growth of Billingham and its increased opportunities for business development. This is the new shop premises which had opened in 1904. The horse and cart, which was such a familiar sight in the district before the First World War, has been replaced by a new delivery van.

This close-up of the north-west corner of Billingham Green is dominated by Cooper's Grocery Shop. It can be compared with the view from chapter one of the Ship Inn, which occupied this same building until 1908.

This garage was originally an eighteenth-century building occupied by a number of businesses before Charlie Poole converted it in 1920 to the first garage to operate in the village. The image provides a fine view of the cottages that stood in Church Row, also built in the eighteenth century. One of these had been used as the village post office before the First World War.

This view shows the original turnpike trust road from Norton to Billingham Bank built in 1789. It also shows the new housing development along Hill Road and Bank Road off Billingham Bank. These were 'staff houses' for employees of Synthetic Ammonia & Nitrates Ltd. Four were completed by mid-1926 whilst a further seven were built on Bank Road in 1927 by Lumsdens of Newcastle. This view can be compared with a similar view in chapter two taken before the housing development was built.

This image is from the 1930s and shows two significant road developments. The inset shows Billingham Bank, widened in October 1929 following a request from the council in 1928 for this work to be done with some urgency. The other development is Billingham Bypass which opened in the 1930s and is seen here in front of the houses built around Hill Road.

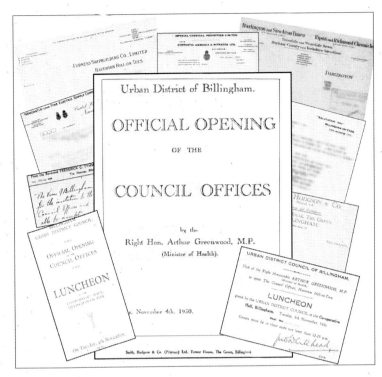

The expansion of Billingham was officially marked with the opening in 1930 of new council offices in Haverton Hill, still considered the focal point of the area. This was a far cry from the days when the first meetings of the old parish council had been held in a school classroom. It was reported as being a 'splendid day' and some of the ephemera from the occasion are shown here.

The population of Billingham in 1931 was 17,972, an increase of 10,000 in ten years. This resulted in a massive expansion in the number of new houses being built. These were mainly council or company housing schemes but there were also some private estates too. Between 1925 and 1933 1,600 houses were built. Initially this was in the area between the village and the station, but it soon spread north of the station too. The new developments received a great deal of praise in the local newspapers, as shown in the insets, with Central Avenue, shown here, hailed as an example of 'excellent town planning'.

Billingham South Works (renamed Cassel Works in 1939) opened in March 1930, part of ICI's continued expansion. The local workforce was joined by men from companies like Castner Kellner Alkali in Wallsend, United Alkali in Gateshead and Cassel Cyanide in Glasgow. Special trains brought families to a village they had never heard of where they were escorted the short distance to their new homes by pipers. Some houses were barely completed. Often they had to walk on planks to reach their new homes as paths were not yet laid. The area around Malvern Road (shown here) and Cotswold Crescent became known as 'Scotch Town'. The nearest school was some distance away in old Billingham until Pentland School opened in June 1938, its new headmistress was Miss Sarah Roxby.

The housing expansion continued throughout the 1930s. Private companies built properties like these (here by Harland and Parker in 1935) at High Grange Estate. This was on land belonging to Billingham High Grange Farm, owned by Freddie Bell, whose family had mixed feelings as they watched more and more of their land being taken over for building. By 1937 building had extended to the newly opened Swan Hotel where the Monkseaton Estate was being built.

Opinions of the newcomers among the old community were divided. Some didn't welcome the expansion, whilst others saw it as an opportunity for progress, both personal and corporate. Integration was slow for many people. Meanwhile, regular village events continued to be held, such as this garden fête in the grounds of Billingham Hall in August 1922 in aid of St John's Roman Catholic church.

Opposite above: This is an excellent view from the church tower looking across Billingham in 1926. It clearly shows the ongoing construction of the factory, particularly the new main offices which are in the middle of the image. The old village green can also be seen with the open farmland and hedgerows behind it. The road to the left of Brewery House chimney is Belasis Lane. In the far distance Teesmouth can be seen.

Opposite below: This view, looking north from the church tower in the early 1930s, shows the extent to which new housing had filled up the area towards the station. Development had already gone beyond Billingham Station and was now filling up the open land between there and Wolviston. Only the Second World War would bring a halt to this expansion before it was resumed in the post-war period.

Progress often brings changes to the landscape, and a major transformation was the demolition of Billingham Hall in 1935 to make way for Conifer Crescent, a housing development built by Kendrews (Builders) Ltd from Middlesbrough. Here the Hall can be seen in its last years; this image featured in a newspaper report which highlighted the loss of large houses across the Teesside area. The builders agreed to leave the strip of land adjacent to the road and its much admired belt of trees, along with the old lodge which stood at the entrance to the Hall. Both are now the only evidence that Billingham Hall ever existed.

Opposite above: Changes also came to the village itself. In March 1939 it was announced that these old eighteenth-century cottages with red coloured walls situated in Church Road were to be demolished after they were condemned as unfit for habitation. Described as having 'huge low-built rafters... carved from oak... taken from old wind jammers', they had once been part of a farm attached to the church, of which the houses were the actual farmhouse. The cottage on the left was the old post office before the First World War (see chapter one).

Opposite below: In 1938 the chairman of the council, A.T.S. Zealley stated that Billingham had grown at an abnormal rate bringing desperate demand for housing and other facilities. One major problem resulting from the sheer number of people who came each day to work in the Billingham area was the increase in traffic, particularly at Billingham Station. These images from the late 1930s show the problem; they also show how busy Billingham Station could be. The remaining image shows Station Road in a quieter moment in the late 1930s.

18th Century Cottages at Billingham

Traffic from Stockton

Traffic from Wolviston

In January 1929, a United bus was hit by a train as it crossed the line at Billingham Station. There were no serious injuries but, as can be seen, the spectacular event attracted front-page press coverage.

Like Billingham Station, the crossing at Belasis Halt also caused traffic problems. This was where the railway from Billingham to Haverton Hill crossed Belasis Lane. It can be seen on many aerial images just north of the Synthetic Ammonia & Nitrates Ltd factory. The halt was so narrow that a small bus could only just pass through. This problem was finally solved in 1937 with the building of the bridge that remains there today.

This aerial view from around 1930 shows how the factory site had expanded by this time. The housing developments around Roscoe Road and Central Avenue can be seen, as can the old winding lane that went to Cowpen Bewley. The new main offices are shown, as is the new Synthonia Club. Most notable of all, however, is the extent of the remaining farmland which had yet to be built on. The inset shows the construction of Billingham Baths in 1934, another new amenity at that time.

As the demand for housing showed little sign of diminishing, the town expanded further from its original centre. In 1930 the council began the building of their Cowpen Lane Estate. These views were taken during the alteration of the old winding lane from Cowpen Bewley into a modern road. The images are: the top of Central Avenue (top left),

looking towards the Synthonia Club (top right), looking from Cowpen Lane crossing towards Billingham South School (bottom left) and the Cowpen Lane gate crossing replaced by a bridge (bottom right).

By the early 1930s the need for a bridge across the Tees became increasingly apparent to link the rapidly developing north bank with Middlesbrough and its environs. Legislation and plans to cross the river at Newport, linking with a new road on the north bank – and thus with Billingham – were agreed. Newport Bridge was opened by the Duke and Duchess of York in 1934. The top left and top right images look towards Billingham; one showing the new link road and the other Billingham Beck. The bottom images are views taken west of the bridge, showing it before and after the construction of the main upright sections.

To conclude this chapter, it is good to see that at least one local pastime hadn't disappeared. For many years, Billingham Bottoms attracted skaters during severe winters. People came from as far away as Hartlepool (see chapter three) and local millers rented out skates and sledges, whilst local traders selling hot food set up their stands either at Chapel Road (Billingham) or Mill Lane (Norton). Flooding across the Bottoms could be extensive and there was a large area available for skaters when it froze. These images from the 1930s show its popularity.

6

ON THE MAP

ICI was undeniably a major force in the development of twentieth-century Billingham. Whilst the company had its critics and many criticisms were justifiably made, ICI's commitment to the welfare of its employees and their families is beyond doubt. Not only did they offer modern, well-built homes for their workers, but they also provided various facilities for their social and leisure activities too. One example, shown here shortly after its construction, was the Synthonia Club, which offered a variety of activities for young and old.

Chiltons Lane 1926

Several projects ancillary to the design and erection of plants were on-going in the mid-1920s. A major scheme was the construction of the main offices in Chilton's Lane on a meadow in front of the Research Buildings. Work was begun by Lumsdens of Newcastle in 1926. The offices were fully occupied by May 1927. They offered much-improved office facilities for the staff and, in the opinion of many, reflected the ever-increasing status of the company. This view looks towards the village with the church and Brewery House visible. In the far distance the development at Billingham Station is just visible whilst new housing adjacent to Chilton's Lane is in the foreground.

Opposite above: With No. 2 unit operational there was no time to stand still. By January 1924 the sulphate plant was operational and by 1925 'systematic development of the site with plants capable of indefinite expansion was being planned'. Within five years the factory would be acclaimed as one of the world's largest with an output of 2,000 tons of nitrate per day. No. 3 unit was operational by early 1928 and Nos 4 and 5 units were to follow. This view from around 1925 looks north to the Haverton Road with another phase of construction underway next to the boiler plant.

Opposite below: Detailed knowledge of the presence of anhydrite was not known when the site was purchased in 1920 and the mining of such an essential raw material *in situ* was not foreseen. However, a 28ft seam of anhydrite was proved in November 1925 and discussions on mining at Billingham began in December. The mining of anhydrite would prove to be of invaluable use to the company and has been called a 'gift of the gods'. This is the head of the shaft and was taken on 30 December 1926. It was closed in 1971.

This image and the one following are both from the mid-1920s and illustrate the sheer scale of the factory expansion. This view shows in some detail just how the area around Billingham Grange has changed and been developed. The gardens at the farm have gone; the original farmhouse is dwarfed by new buildings all around it. Old Chilton's Lane can still be seen, but only a solitary tree and bits of hedgerow show it was ever a country lane.

This aerial view from the mid-1920s exemplifies still further the massive changes that had taken place. The Grange is now almost lost amidst a sea of industrial plants and buildings. The position of the farmhouse is indicated, but there is very little else to be recognised of the site prior to the advent of Synthetic Ammonia & Nitrates Ltd.

Late in 1926 it became known that Brunner Mond, the United Alkali Co., Nobel Industries of Ardeer and the British Dyestuffs Corporation of Blackley were to merge and the name ICI was registered on 7 December 1926. Synthonia Ammonia & Nitrates Ltd continued as a separately run subsidiary, with a management executive of seven led by Dr Roland Slade. George Pollitt was elected to the new board and ceased to have full-time responsibility at Billingham. This image from around 1926 shows the main office near completion with the temporary huts used by workmen still visible.

This view of the 'Synthetic Works' (as it was known locally) is taken from the main offices looking east into the factory itself, *c.* 1928. It's useful to compare this with the view in chapter four of Chilton's Lane taken only eight years previously. A rural lane bordered by fields and haystacks and not much wider than a cart track has been developed into a main road in the middle of an industrial complex.

This aerial view from around 1928-29 shows Billingham South Works under construction. New Road is now complete, dividing the industrial complex into north and south sites. This image is particularly special as very few images exist which show Brook House Farm. Almost equally rare are images of Billingham Mill which, like the Mill Race, is visible here. Both were demolished shortly after this picture was taken as the factory expanded.

Opposite above: This aerial view shows Tibbersley Farm in its final days. Like Billingham Grange, it too has been dwarfed by the industrial developments springing up around it. The junction of the newly completed New Road and Haverton Hill Road is also shown with the British Oxygen site visible too.

Opposite below: This image shows a group of workers who were employed in the new Billingham South Works when the sodium plant began operations at 6.28 a.m. on Tuesday 1 April 1930. Construction was still ongoing all around the plant as gradually more and more plants came online. Many of the men employed in the sodium plant had come from the Castner-Kellner Company's Wallsend works and had only recently arrived in Billingham with their families. For many it was a case of new job, new home and new life having moved from a busy town like Wallsend to Billingham (then still a comparatively rural backwater).

Tibbersley Farm

New Road

Haverton Hill Road

Both Synthetic Ammonia & Nitrates Ltd and ICI were renowned for the care they showed for their employees, typified by their local housing schemes. They also promoted recreational facilities for their workforce. The first Synthonia Club, a temporary building opened in 1922, is shown on the top left. A replacement was opened in 1930 by Lord Melchett, chairman of ICI (top right), and he is presented with a book (bottom right). The opening of the Synthonia Bowling Green by Dr Roland Slade is shown in the inset bottom left, as are programmes for two of the productions by the Synthonia Players.

The facilities available to employees are well illustrated here with views of the Synthonia Club and one of the Synthonia Scouts from the 1930s. A lot of activities were centred on the club including Synthonia Scouts, the Synthonia Boys' Club and a thriving theatrical group. A main playing field was laid in July 1927; tennis courts in October 1927, a bowling green in July 1928 and a cricket pitch in July 1929. ICI also supported Billingham South (later Synthonia) Football Club who gained admission, in 1937, to the Northern (Football) League, and the Synthonia Cricket Club, which gained admission to the North Yorkshire and South Durham Cricket League in 1931.

Works' outings were another feature of life for employees and they enjoyed many trips during the years they worked for ICI and previously for Synthetic Ammonia & Nitrates Ltd. This image shows one such outing for Synthetic Ammonia & Nitrates Ltd employees. In June 1928 a day trip travelled to Ullswater in the Lake District, a scenic destination far removed from these employees' busy working lives in the factory.

Another outing can be seen here in 1935 with this group of ICI employees and their families awaiting the train at Billingham Station. As the train is approaching from the west, this is probably a trip to the coast at Seaton Carew, a popular seaside destination.

The success of Synthetic Ammonia & Nitrates Ltd and later ICI brought a number of prestigious visitors to see the factory. One memorable visitor was the Prince of Wales, later Edward VIII, on 2 July 1930. After visiting Middlesbrough, the Prince crossed the Tees to Billingham, alighting at Bamlett's Wharf, where he was greeted by Lord Londonderry, Lord Lieutenant of County Durham, Lord Melchett, chairman of ICI, and the chief constable of Durham. The Prince then met directors of Synthetic Ammonia & Nitrates Ltd before he toured the factory. He also visited the new Synthonia Club and the main offices where he was cheered by large crowds. The Prince finished his day with a round of golf at Seaton Carew Golf Club!

A less publicised royal visit took place during the Second World War on 19 June 1941 when H.R.H. King George VI and H.R.H. Queen Elizabeth visited ICI Billingham. Here they are seen with Dr Alexander Fleck, who came to ICI Billingham in 1927. Dr Fleck later rose to become ICI's chairman from 1953-1960 and was created a baron in 1961. In 1932 the number of workers at Billingham was 5,000, and by 1944 it had risen to 11,000.

Another very famous visitor was George Bernard Shaw, who came to ICI Billingham on 22 June 1931. A guest of Dr Roland Slade, Shaw stayed overnight at Hardwick Hall, Norton before his factory visit. He also toured the Synthonia Club where he sang the tonic sol-fa scale on the theatre stage in order to test its acoustic qualities! He then toured the other facilities and still found time to see some of the housing projects in the area.

Ramsay MacDonald, Prime Minister until May 1935, visited ICI Billingham to officially open the oil works in October 1931. Accompanied by Sir Harry McGowan KBE (ICI's chairman 1930-1950) and the plant manager, Kenneth Gordon, MacDonald commented that he thought the plant was an 'astonishing creation of thought, research and skill.' The main image shows the official party at the opening of the oil works which, as the inset shows, made headline news in local newspapers.

Above and below: Although the developments at Billingham read at times like a *Boys' Own* adventure, it was, in reality, a very dangerous industry. Safety at Synthetic Ammonia & Nitrates Ltd and later at ICI was always of prime consideration. Nethertheless, accidents did happen. As early as April 1924 there was a fatality at the works when a pump-line feed burst, killing the operator. Other major accidents occurred, including the death of eleven employees in 1934 when ammonia escaped, whilst an explosion in April 1940 killed eight men. These were serious accidents and usually made front-page news, but the excellent safety record overall at Synthetic Ammonia & Nitrates Ltd and at ICI throughout the years must be acknowledged.

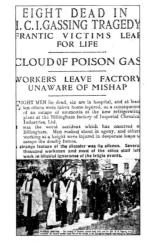

Although Synthetic Ammonia & Nitrates Ltd were well aware of the need for positive industrial relations with their workforce, internal discord was not unknown. ICI, also keen to be proactive in this area, inaugurated in 1929 the first Works Council, a body which aimed to promote discussion rather than conflict. A major influence at this time in protecting workers rights was Eddie Hutton, an instrument artificer who, in 1938, led members of the Amalgamated Engineering Union in an orderly march to Billingham Green – the first major strike at Billingham South Works. He later became chairman of the Workers' Representatives at Central Council.

ICI had always taken care to recognise the contribution made by their employees; such care was exemplified by their long-service award dinners. A group of employees who attended one such event at the Grand Hotel in West Hartlepool in 1955 is shown here. Some of these employees had worked in the chemical industry for thirty-five years, having begun their careers long before the creation of ICI, with companies which no longer existed.

This view, taken in the late 1930s from the church tower, should be compared with that in the previous chapter showing Billingham in 1926 from the same point. Most of the agricultural land has been swallowed up by the factory and the huge housing estates that were still being built. Billingham Green too has changed. In the north-east corner, replacing the old cottages, the newly opened Methodist church is visible. Brewery House, once the dominant building on East Row, has now been demolished.

7

LIFE ON THE FARM

This wonderful image is very evocative of farming in the period between the two world wars. It shows the Dixon family in the late 1920s, out in the fields enjoying their lunch. The wicker picnic basket, the metal jug of tea, the tin cups and even the men themselves, with their waistcoats and dangling pocket-watch chains, are reminiscent of a way of life which few can now recall. In the background even the horses seem to be enjoying their break, with plenty of hay provided for them to eat.

The rapid movement away from agriculture to industry had grave consequences for Billingham's farming community. Many farms lost land or were swept away entirely. One such farm was Billingham High Grange. It lay a quarter of a mile east of the road to Wolviston, just over a mile away from the village where Billingham Town Centre stands today. The farmhouse stood on the site of the technical college which has ironically suffered a similar fate a mere fifty years into its existence. The multi-view shows the farm in the 1930s and it can be seen from all sides.

Billingham High Grange was owned by the Bell family, one of the few farms which were not leased from the Church authorities. The farm was 365 acres in size with a farm house which had six bedrooms, a breakfast room, lounge and a dining room with two windows which looked out to the sea and Teesmouth in the distance. From the lounge they looked across the fields to the railway and the distant church tower in the village. An orchard stood next to the eastern side of the house. This view shows horses, for which the Bell family were renowned, in the field in front of the house, and the new housing development north of the railway can be seen in the distance.

When the First World War began, Freddie Bell lost his favourite horse, 'Little Chilton', to the Army. Bell was paid around £70, considered a very fair price. Freddie Bell, in the lower image, was a special police constable during the war and a church warden in Billingham for twenty-three years. His daughter, Freda Bell, recalled that the bombing of Hartlepool in 1914 lifted the huge barn doors at the farm right off their hinges! One night in 1914 some men from the Ministry of Munitions who were surveying locally came to the farm asking for accommodation. Freda's mother sent them on to Mrs Emmett at Billingham Grange Farm where they stayed. Ironically, this was the first farm whose land was later requisitioned by the Ministry of Munitions! Freda also remembered watching from the farm the shooting down of a Zeppelin over Cargo Fleet in 1917. The upper image shows Alan Bell on his horse at the farm. Like his father, he was a keen horseman.

This image shows ploughing taking place in a field which lies directly behind the Swan Hotel, Billingham. The farmhouse in the background is Wolviston Grange Farm, which was only a couple of fields away from High Grange. In the distance, the newly built houses on the Monkseaton Estate at the Swan Hotel can be seen, *c.* 1938.

A wonderful series of images record farming before the Second World War when the work was very labour intensive and hugely dependent on men and horses. These images record the Dixon family from Glebe Farm in Billingham, who were at the time the champion ploughing family in the whole of Britain. Tom Dixon's father, John, started the tradition by winning no less than seventy-eight championships. Tom carried on the tradition by winning 263 ploughing championships before he retired in 1932. He had come to Billingham in 1904 and spent the rest of his life farming at Glebe Farm and running the Dixon milk round. John and Leslie became the third generation of champions. This first image shows harvesting in 1929 with Tom and Leslie on top of a haystack in a field next to Billingham Hall. Billingham Station and Wolviston Road are in the distance.

Opposite above: A group of farm workers stop for lunch in this wonderful image of rural life in the summer of 1928. The land they farmed stretched from the end of Central Avenue as far as the Swan Hotel. This is the field next to Billingham Station. The station buildings and signal box can be seen in the distance.

Opposite below: Most of the land farmed by the Dixons was some distance from the village so the lunch basket with its jug of tea was often used! The workers (and the dog) are having lunch close to Billingham Hall, observed by a horse nearby. Today it seems remarkable that farm workers would wear a tie and waistcoat to work in the fields. Tom Dixon's watch chain is visible and next to him sits his eldest son, John.

Before 1914 the Dixons usually kept this field next to Billingham Hall as pasture land. However, the need for food meant that it went under the plough and continued to do so even when the war ended. The trees behind the fence are those on the perimeter of the gardens at Billingham Hall, the tower of which can be seen behind the trees. Station Road would be immediately to the right of the photograph. This is a fascinating, nostalgic image of man and horses working together on the land.

Two shire horses plough under the watchful eye of Leslie Dixon, younger son of Tom Dixon. Leslie too won over 100 ploughing championships and represented Britain in competitions in Canada in the 1950s. Leslie was the first Dixon to use the tractor rather than horses to plough.

This image, taken in a field off Sandy Lane, shows men working in the fields in the 1930s; it is interesting because Wolviston Road is in the distance. Greenholme, one of the large detached houses built along there at the start of the century, is just visible.

Until the First World War Sandy Lane was a gated road with one gate near the junction with Wolviston Road and the other just past the junction with the track which led up to Northfield Farm. The first houses on Sandy Lane, shown in the distance here, were built in the late 1920s close to the junction with Wolviston Road. Until the mid-1930s they marked the northern limit of the development of Billingham. Leslie Dixon is shown here driving one of the first tractors owned by the family along Sandy Lane.

Until the 1920s Wolviston Road was a country lane with little development apart from three houses called Greenholme, Ashtree Cottage and Winford House. A small group of houses were built at the top of Sandy Lane in 1929 – these are shown here behind the farm workers. This field too would soon give way to a housing development as Billingham developed ever northwards. The workers include John Dixon (seated).

This is Sandy Lane at harvest time in around 1938 with Tom Dixon looking on from the road and Leslie Dixon on top of the stack. The Dixons had a cow byre near here to save taking the cows back to the village. St Aiden's Crescent is off to the right and Wolviston Road is in the distance.

Tom Dixon started the milk round and his two sons continued it. The horse pulled the milk cart as far as Ashtree Cottage (which was Leslie's last call). The Dixons also delivered milk around the village as well as seven pints each day to Billingham Hall. With over 2,000 customers they bought in milk from neighbouring farms including White House and Wilmire Farms to cope with the demand.

Leslie Dixon was a natural mechanic and had many adventures with his vehicles, including one spectacular crash in his beloved Bullnose Morris in December 1928. He told me that he was collecting milk one morning and 'going tearin' hell for leather down Sandy Lane, with churns, in the pitch dark.' He 'got into a broadside... copped 'er over, tore me ear off and ended up sat in the middle of the road with just the steering wheel in me hand.' Here Leslie is seen in more sedate times with one of the Dixon lorries that were once such a familiar sight in Billingham.

Another wonderful series of images, depicting a way of life that has vanished forever, come from photographer Ivan Harrington. In 1914 his father moved into Brickyard House (formerly used by the brickyard manager), one of two properties located just east of Billingham Junction on a former brickfield. Len Harrington renamed the house 'Pond House.' It is seen here in the summer of 1951.

The same view taken again by Ivan Harrington, but in winter; Len made many alterations to the house during the time the family lived there. The original kilns were still present when the family moved in and outbuildings were made from bricks that were found there.

Ivan Harrington took this close-up view of the house and the NER cottage which stood further down towards the railway junction. The NER cottage was demolished in 1954.

This image of his parents Len and Hilda Harrington, along with their sister-in-law Ginny, was also taken by Ivan Harrington during a family mealtime at Pond House. Life at the house must have been very difficult at times with no electricity. Ivan recalls an occasion during the Second World War when a bomb dropped during the night. It exploded only a few hundred yards away on the opposite side of the line and woke everyone up with a start. Incidentally, the door seen in the background came from Billingham Hall having been bought by Len when the Hall was demolished.

This multi-image, again from Ivan Harrington, shows, on the left, Len and his sister Ivy Harrington with a family friend in around 1923 in front of Pond House. The image looks towards open countryside that would become, within a decade, part of the Cowpen Housing Estate. The other image shows Len Harrington at the back of Pond House putting in a window which had come from Billingham Hall when it was demolished!

8

EXPANDING AGAIN

Billingham 1960's

Modern Billingham is reflected in this image. It shows Billingham Town Centre in the mid-1960s, during the Billingham International Folklore Festival. Large crowds watch as an outdoor concert is performed whilst in the distance, construction of the Town Centre continues. The Town Centre is very much of its time, a post-war world when a new style of simple architecture was adopted, with pedestrianised shopping areas accessible to all, well serviced by local transport and car parks. This was the culmination of the efforts of Billingham Council to provide a post-war town of which the citizens could be proud. Forty years on, the festival remains an enduring success; but for the Town Centre, time has moved on, the star of the 1960s has risen and fallen, overtaken by new developments elsewhere in the region.

Billingham Green, seen here after the Second World War, can be compared with the image in chapter one taken from almost the same place. Apart from the loss of Brewery House, no obvious changes are apparent. The road still divides Billingham Green, the schoolmaster's house and adjacent farmhouse are both still standing but the image has a 'busy feel' about it. Perhaps this is because the village green is now just a small part of a growing town.

Demolition of High Grange Farm

The Bell family, who farmed at Billingham High Grange, felt the loss of their land keenly. For a decade they watched the gradual encroachment of the new housing estates before they finally left the farm altogether. These images show the last ever crop being sown on the fields which were soon to become part of the new town centre. The second image records the demolition of the farm buildings. The loss of the eighteenth-century farmhouse was a particular tragedy. Ironically, only the house built for their hind in 1903 still remains today. A new technical college was built on the site of the farm buildings.

The development of Billingham continued after the Second World War. The new road had opened which bypassed Billingham Station and its problematic traffic bottleneck. It also opened up land north of the station. Plans for a new commercial focus in Billingham were soon put into operation after 1945. This post-war development began to attract national attention. The new, totally modern town centre was the 'jewel in the crown' and this image from around 1953 shows construction well under way. The new park, named after John Whitehead, former clerk to the council who died suddenly in 1948, is being laid in the distance. The insets show contemporary press coverage.

Under John Whitehead's successor, Fred Dawson, the council decided to build a new town with living facilities 'second to none' in Britain. In 1951 the town was granted a coat of arms with the motto 'Faith', chosen to represent faith in Billingham and the industries which supported it. A new shopping centre was begun in 1953. It was centred on Queensway, a main thoroughfare which allowed close access to the shopping area. With its open-plan approach and clean-cut style of architecture, it was far removed from the old village shops at Billingham Green. A new kind of shopping experience was being offered which aimed not only to be a convenient alternative for local residents but also to compete with existing centres such as Stockton and Middlesbrough.

Left: This image from 1960 will be familiar to local residents who will recall many of these shop names. Shopping in Queensway with its broad, paved areas was a very different experience to that of the narrow, crowded streets of towns like Middlesbrough. Other facilities were also being offered including a new public library just to the north of the shopping centre.

Below: Queensway itself was the main thoroughfare with the local bus service dropping passengers close to the new town centre. It soon proved to be a huge success with local people and even brought in people from farther afield. The 1960s was seen as an age for young people with their modern way of living and Billingham reflected this style, being perceived as a modern town for modern people.

With the huge ICI factory bearing its name, Billingham became a town known across the country. The progressive Billingham Council decided to build an enclosed pedestrian precinct based on what they had seen during a visit to the rebuilt city of Coventry in 1959. In the early 1960s a new two-level shopping block and a two-tiered car park were built. Further development followed, culminating in the opening of the West Precinct in 1967. This development contained two-storey shopping facilities, an imposing office block, a night club and a pub. The circular pram ramp shown here exemplifies the people-friendly approach and epitomises the style of the 1960s architecture.

The introduction of the annual Billingham Folklore Festival quickly attracted local praise as well as attention from far beyond the region. It continues to be a huge success today, and its week of festivities brings many people into the town from far and wide. This image is from the festival in 1966.

It was the age of 'the new', as shown by this multi-view. Top left is Billingham Campus, a school at the forefront of education which integrated grammar and secondary modern schools as Britain moved towards educational equality. The image on the top right shows the building of Billingham Forum, an innovative approach to leisure which combined sports and theatre facilities in the same complex. The Billingham Arms Hotel opened in 1958 and greatly enhanced the facilities offered by the town centre. Finally, bottom right, Maureen Taylor, a local councillor, declares the John Whitehead Park open in 1957, a green, landscaped leisure area for the town's people.

Opposite above: Another new building which attracted national attention was the state-of-the-art Synthonia Sports Stadium. A grand opening by the Earl of Derby took place on 6 September 1958. As a purpose-built modern stadium with floodlights, it held both national and international athletics events and became the home of Billingham Synthonia Football Club. Other high-profile users included the England football team, who trained there in the early 1960s.

Opposite below: An international athletics match in 1963 between Great Britain and the Benelux Countries was held at Synthonia Stadium. This event was televised live by the BBC as part of their *Grandstand* programme with David Coleman commentating. In the distance the brand new ICI main offices can be seen. High profile visits in the 1960s by the Queen and the Duke of Edinburgh were all part of the national recognition being given to Billingham at this time. The Council had indeed fulfilled their aims and the town, very definitely, 'had arrived'.

Northern Counties
Athletic Association
(ESTABLISHED 1879)

★

PROGRAMME OF

THE ANNUAL

Championships

at the

BILLINGHAM SYNTHONIA STADIUM
CENTRAL AVENUE, BILLINGHAM
(by kind permission)

Saturday, 23rd June, 1962
Commencing at 1.15 p.m.

★

Programme Sixpence

SYNTHONIA
SPORTSFIELD OPENING

The next two aerial views from the early 1960s show most of the post-war major development of Billingham at that time. The new buildings of the Stockton and Billingham Technical College are visible in the centre, as is Billingham Town Centre complete with its new tenpin bowling alley. The council fulfilled its promise to build new houses after the cessation of building during the war and many of them are visible in this image. Privately owned housing also boomed and the substantial development west of the A19 is also shown here. It was to expand substantially more in the late 1960s, consuming much of the remaining farmland shown in this image.

This view looks over the housing built close to Roseberry Road in the mid-1950s towards Marsh House Avenue. The new Billingham Campus School is under construction in the distance. Originally in 1958, only one school occupied this site before three others were added to it. With its own swimming pool and dedicated science and technology buildings, it was considered very innovative. However, it was reorganised as a comprehensive school in 1972. The grammar school building, Bede Hall, was later demolished in the 1980s. The farmland seen here would all be developed in the 1970s and 1980s.

The expansion of Billingham at this time wasn't just about building on farmland. This was the 1960s and although well meaning, the desire to build new houses sometimes failed to recognise less tangible qualities that existed within the old communities. With seemingly undue haste, town councils and planners tore down old properties and replaced them with 'modern', concrete buildings which, although adequate for their purpose, often did little to retain the ambience and spirit of the old communities. Billingham Green was an example of this approach. A grey, sombre winter's day seems only to emphasise the sorrow felt by many at the demolition of old Billingham.

This view shows the former site of North Row after the cottages have been demolished in the 1960s. New, flat-roofed, modern buildings would soon fill these empty spaces but for now the old schoolmaster's house and the Methodist church stand alone. Both buildings would also be demolished later.

The new housing at North Row on Billingham Green is shown here in 1984. The Methodist church remains, but the only eighteenth-century property remaining on East Row is the old farmhouse. Compare this view with earlier images.

ICI continued its success although few realised when this image was taken in around 1960 that these would be their halcyon years. This view is of Nitrates Avenue and the Grange farmhouse, which was then in use as a medical centre.

Two hundred years of history came to an end in 1982 when the Grange farmhouse was demolished by ICI amidst cries of protest. Seen here in around 1975, in its final days, it was the last reminder of the site's rural history. Some people could still remember it as a working farmhouse, but time had eventually caught up with it, as indeed it finally did with the company itself.

Once considered an iconic symbol of the success of Synthetic Ammonia & Nitrates Ltd and later of ICI, the main offices, known as 'Chilton House', were demolished in 1998. These images by Ivan Harrington capture the event as the machines go to work. For many this was the end of an era, just as the original building of the offices and the loss of Chilton's Lane had been for the villagers of Billingham. Ironically, the offices built to replace Chilton House are today, in 2008, awaiting demolition and ICI itself is no longer a presence in Billingham. Time, it seems, has moved on.

The Billingham Station bottleneck had been solved by the opening in 1944 of a bypass west of the station. This view looks towards Billingham Station. It is taken from the Davies Bridge which crosses the railway to the west of the station. It offers a complete vista of the station buildings together with the coal depot. In the distance the Station Hotel and the housing erected in the 1930s can also be seen. The field on the immediate right is now a housing estate and those knowledgeable about railways will note the old wooden gates still in use at the crossing.

Billingham Station had been built in 1866 replacing an earlier structure. Now, a century later, in 1966 it too was replaced by a new station built just north of Roseberry Bridge. This location was considered to be more advantageous in serving the people of Billingham, although ironically there have recently been rumours of plans to create a rail halt back on the site of the old station!

Billingham continued to expand northwards. Building west of the old A19 at the Swan Hotel began in the 1930s but was halted by the Second World War. Grosvenor Road in 1937-38 is shown on the top left; top right is Wolviston Road (then the A19) in the 1950s looking south from the end of Jubilee Grove. As traffic increased, work is shown, bottom left, widening Wolviston Road in 1957. Next to it is Wolviston Road, again in the 1950s, looking north to Wolviston. At the time these properties were located on the northern edge of Billingham.

These four images illustrating simple family life reflect the result of Billingham's development for the ordinary people of the town. The upper two images are taken in 1962 at Carlton Avenue on Wolviston Court Estate, then a single line of bungalows looking out across fields to Wolviston. The fields will soon be gone to be replaced by yet more housing. They show a mother and her children happily at play. The lower two are taken in the 1950s in a back garden in Northfield Road. The open view in the image on the left has become part of Wilmire Road, the new houses visible behind the small boy joyfully kicking a ball around in the image on the right!

Other local titles published by The History Press

A Century of Stockton-on-Tees
CHARLIE EMETT

This fascinating selection of more than 180 photographs illustrates the extraordinary transformations that have taken place in Stockton-on-Tees during the twentieth century. Many aspects of Stockton's recent history are covered, famous occasions and individuals are remembered and the impact of national and international events are witnessed in this nostalgic selection which will delight locals and visitors alike.

978 07509 4910 1

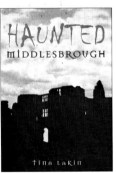

Around Billingham
VERA CHAPMAN

Billingham village, a Saxon settlement of seventh-century origin nestled beside village green and Saxon church, retained a rural identity until the First World War. When hostilities ended, ICI was formed, and became a feature of the area. The fascinating photographs which comprise this nostalgic volume illustrate these dramatic confrontations.

978 18458 8251 8

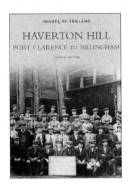

Haunted Middlesbrough
TINA LAKIN

This terrifying collection of true-life tales takes the reader on a tour through the attics, cemeteries, streets and houses of the region. Containing all manner of spooky goings-ons, this collection will delight all lovers of a good ghost story.

978 07524 4193 1

Haverton Hill Port Clarence to Billingham
COLIN H. HATTON

This nostalgic collection of more than 180 images celebrates life in the area as it used to be. School days, work, celebrations and disasters – every aspect of life in the region is here in this delightful collection which will be enjoyed by visitors and residents alike.

978 07524 3425 4

If you are interested in purchasing other books published by The History Press, or in case you have difficulty finding any History Press books in your local bookshop, you can also place orders directly through our website

www.thehistorypress.co.uk